GETTING DIGITAL MARKETING *RIGHT*

For my parents,
DAVID AND GINGER BRADLEY,
who taught me about hard work, drive, and love.

For my girlfriend,
SAHONNY NUNEZ,
who endlessly supports my dreams.

And for my fellow entrepreneurs,
who deserve to reach their own dreams.

Contents

GETTING DIGITAL MARKETING *RIGHT*

A Simplified Process for Business Growth, Goal Attainment, and Powerful Marketing

David J. Bradley

PREFACE

Why You Need This Book

I want to thank and congratulate you for investing in this digital marketing strategy book.

I wrote this book to help people understand how to approach digital marketing in a simple, comprehensive, and impactful way.

But who exactly is it for?

- **Students** who found that their college studies neglected to cover the exponential growth of digital marketing.
- **Marketers** who know about tactics, like social media, pay-per-click, and email marketing, but don't know how to design a strategy that uses the best tactics for a specific purpose.

- **Business owners** who are looking to lead their business into an effective, digital strategy focused on their vision and goals.
- **Freelance experts** who know their trade, whether copywriting, web design, or social media, but need to understand how they fit into the big picture to better serve their clients and demand more money for their projects.

Digital marketing is limited when you only focus on individual tactics, rather than the overall plan. It's like when you build your business… If you only focus on your product, you're dead before you begin. What about your competitors? Customer expectations? Budget?

Even if you're an expert SEO guy, or an amazing designer, or an "advertising guru", without knowing how to incorporate it into a strategy, you're limited. And since most of us are probably not an expert in a tactic like that, it becomes even more important to know strategy.

We want to focus on results. We don't need to know how to be experts in a certain tactic, so that won't be covered in this book. If you want to know how to become great at web design, copywriting, SEO, or so on, there's thousands of great resources online.

For everyone else, if you just want to know how to design a strategy that delivers return-on-investment and can be used regardless of your technical skills and abilities, keep on reading.

Yes, it's beyond business.

In this book, you will learn proven steps to crafting a powerful strategy to reach your personal and business goals.

We aren't mindless drones, tuned for maximal output. We have interests, emotions, goals, and needs. Whatever category you fit into: entrepreneur, employee, freelancer; you are in business for personal reasons.

> Is your business going to be automated one day so that you can travel the world?
>
> Do you want to climb the corporate ladder until you reach the pinnacle as CEO of your organization?
>
> Are you looking to earn enough money to work less hours and still maintain your ideal lifestyle?

Being able to understand, create, implement, and measure a strategy in today's fastest growing marketing medium can help you reach any of those goals.

Even more personal.

I've used this framework outside of digital marketing as well. It isn't something to be kept in a silo. When you're done with it all, look back at the general structure and see how it can apply to other parts of your life.

The framework helped me to discover what fueled me, and what limited me. It helped me to remove harmful parts of my life and focus on healthy, fulfilling opportunities. It's what helped me to take the plunge by starting my own business.

I believe looking at concepts and frameworks in a cross-disciplinary way leads to growth in all areas of your life.

But, back to the focus…

Digital marketing is still a relatively new medium.

It's filled with amazing opportunities and a continuous stream of new marketing services and tactics.

In writing this book alone, I discovered dozens of new options for me to choose from to market my book.

Seriously, think about it. How many different skills come to mind when you think of "digital marketing"?

- Google AdWords
- PPC Advertising
- Press Releases
- Search Engine Marketing
- Search Engine Optimization
- Keyword Research
- Landing Pages
- Blogging
- Content Marketing
- Lead Capture Forms
- Social Media Marketing
- Facebook
- Twitter
- Google+
- LinkedIn
- Instagram
- Pinterest
- Copywriting
- eCommerce
- Web Design
- Mobile-Responsive
- Affiliate Marketing
- Autoresponders
- Email Marketing
- Video Marketing
- CRM Systems
- Display Ads
- Podcasting
- Graphic Design

- Text Message Marketing
- Retargeting
- Site Programming

And the list can go on…

But having expertise in all these different areas isn't what's important.

What's important is to understand how each area can be leveraged to get you closer to your goals. To paraphrase Bruce Lee, "absorb what is useful; discard what is not."

Creating and implementing a strategy allows you to do just that. You use the right elements of digital marketing to help you reach your target goals. In fact, without a strategy, being an expert in any of these areas is extremely limiting, unless you are guided by a strategist. Perhaps, you will be that strategist soon enough.

Again, I found this framework incredibly useful myself. It's the same thing I use with my clients and my own business to make sure we are headed in the right direction.

By the end of this book, you are going to be able to form digital marketing strategies, teach them to others, reach your goals, and ultimately make your dreams a reality.

Throughout the book, you'll notice action steps. Please, take action. Action is needed if you want this to really pay off. Apply what you learn, and I'm confident this will help your business. Besides, if you're going to invest the time to read this book, you might as well invest it wisely.

Follow the framework, take action, and you'll see that digital marketing can be the catalyst to exponential growth. If you have a steady business and at least some budget to invest, I think you'll enjoy the return-on-investment, increased efficiency, and goals you accomplish after reading this book.

Enough talking… Let's get to work!

P.S. Thanks again for investing in this book – I hope you enjoy it!

FAQ – Skeptics, Read This

Is a digital marketing strategy really necessary? Is it right for me? I'll say *absolutely* now, but if you need more convincing, let's look at some common concerns:

Do I need a big budget for this to be worth it?

There's a huge disparity between the budgets of startups (*minimal*), established small and medium-sized businesses (*plenty*), and large corporations (*ridiculous*).

This book isn't set for a specific budget range, but it mainly helps established small and medium-sized businesses. If you're a startup, you can use this framework to combine efficiency and effectiveness, even with minimal budget

A key to my work with companies is *return-on-investment*. If we can't predict one before we begin the project, I won't even have my client make the investment. We'll try to figure out an alternative for them to look into. With the right methodology, you can do the same, avoiding bad investments and making smart ones.

Do I have to be tech-savvy or a designer?

I'm a pretty tech-savvy guy. I built my own computers and websites. I dabbled in Photoshop and WordPress code. But, for me to really attempt to design or code something leads to two issues:

(a) it will be awful compared to what even an affordable expert can do, and

(b) it'll take time away from what I really am great at.

Leonardo da Vinci once said, "Simplicity is the ultimate sophistication." You'll see this book keeps concepts simple, focusing on why you would want certain tactics and what your overall plan is. We don't get lost in the technical aspects. We just want results.

As you know, part of success is knowing how and when to delegate. Everyone is limited in their time, energy, and abilities. There's things in your business you just won't be able to do. I hope you feel that way about most of what we will cover in this book (except for the strategy, of course).

When it comes to redesigning your website, installing analytics, or optimizing your site to appear in search results, find a professional. It's a small investment for a huge pay off, once you invest the time into making sure your strategy is there to support those tactics.

You have countless options with skilled freelancers on sites like oDesk or Elance, as well as local and international agencies that can help you. Let's just get to the book so you know what team you're going to need to build.

I'm not an MBA. I'm sort of a newbie to digital marketing. Am I ready?...

Don't worry about "credentials" or experience. Like I mentioned, this book keeps things simple (you know, *the ultimate sophistication*). It really isn't about digital marketing; it's about building a strategy. I promise, you *can* and *will* be able to do that.

As long as you invest your time and energy into this, you'll find success. Complete the action steps as they're given to you. You'll not only create a killer strategy, but you'll have a framework to use for the rest of your life (no charge for that bonus!).

Not trying to brag, but I'm pretty darn good at this digital marketing stuff. What's in it for me?

Being an expert sucks. It gets boring and limiting.

There's a concept in Buddhism called "Beginner's Mind" (or Shoshin). It translates just like you might guess, to engage in activities as if you were a beginner. When you're a beginner, you're excited, alive, and eager to learn.

I still try to do this in areas that I'm an expert in, but it can be tough. You need to avoid assumptions and be mindful of when your expert-self is limiting you from the full experience.

And again, it isn't about digital marketing really. It's about strategy, which can benefit just about everyone.

For more on Beginner's Mind, see this article: http://zenhabits.net/how-to-live-life-to-the-max-with-beginners-mind/.

If you still aren't sure, go to the next page and try the short questionnaire. It'll rank your needs based on seven simple, but important questions.

Are you sure I need this?

Okay, I'll play along. Maybe you have all this stuff figured out?

Well, why don't you go through this quiz below and see how you score. This will help us see where you are at the start of this book. We'll revisit this when you complete the book as well.

Do you have a digital marketing strategy? (A detailed plan, written out?)				
No – 0	1	2	3	4 – Yes
We do tactics like email marketing and social media, but no plan.	We know we need a plan, but nothing is in place yet.	We have strategies on some channels, but not overall.	Yes, focused on gaining visitors and converting them into leads.	Yes, we have a plan that includes all our marketing.

Do you track analytics, goals, and key performance indicators?				
No – 0	1	2	3	4 – Yes
We generally leave it to what's worked traditionally.	We check on traffic and keep an eye out for lead increases.	We use Google Analytics, but don't keep track of KPIs.	We use analytics and track goals, but something's missing...	Yes, we use goals, analytics, and KPIs. It's clear how they work together.

Do you speak to a general audience (opposed to a specific, ideal customer)?				
No – 0	1	2	3	4 – Yes
We focus on our products and services. They speak for themselves.	We know generally who we sell to. That's good enough.	We focus on certain targets specifically.	We created a detailed outline of who the buyer is.	We have an in-depth profile of our ideal customers and focus on them.

Do you have a digital sales funnel clearly defined and in use?				
No – 0	1	2	3	4 – Yes
We have salespeople who handle that.	Our phone number and "contact us" form is online so customers can reach us.	We have a rough framework, but we need to build on it.	We spent time developing the digital sales funnel, but not an entire digital strategy.	We have a complete digital sales funnel that integrates with our strategy.

Do you periodically review your digital strategy to improve it?				
No – 0	1	2	3	4 – Yes
We don't have a strategy to review!	We don't have any schedule to review. We will notice when we need to.	Part of our annual plan is to check in on this. I wouldn't say we "set it and forget it".	We constantly work on it, so a schedule isn't set but we think about it.	Our team has a set schedule to check on our strategy and continually improve it.

Are you happy with your budgeting for your digital marketing?				
No – 0	1	2	3	4 – Yes
It gives me headaches trying to decide on a budget, or stick to one.	We set budgets, but that doesn't mean we stick to them.	I feel like we limit ourselves with our budgeting.	We have budgets set up but are unsure if they are best for our needs.	We set smart budgets based on need and performance – all goes well!

Are you positioned well in your market, while making that clear to clients?				
No – 0	1	2	3	4 – Yes
We give info as to who we are... That's about it.	We give information about our products/services offered.	Some web pages explain why we are great to work with.	We try a bunch of messages to communicate our benefits.	Yes, we speak to our ideal customer, in a clear, well-positioned way.

Now, add them up and calculate your total. Where do you land?

0 – 7: Pretty weak, sorry! You got work to do, but this means you have a lot to improve on and benefit from this book.

8 – 14: It seems like you've put energy towards this, but you aren't quite gaining the traction you need to see success. I hope the concepts in this book will at least double your score. (And even more if you do all the exercises.)

15 – 21: Good work! It seems like you've made some great progress and worked to refine your digital marketing. However, as you know, there's room for improvement. 1% improvements make the difference between great and elite athletes. The same is true for businesses, so let's help you be elite.

22 – 28: Okay, you've got it all figured out, huh? Seriously, congratulations! You're ahead of many. Don't worry though, I'm confident you will still benefit from this book. It'll help you build a framework and squeeze your way into a solid score of 28!

Did you find that fun? Interesting? Informative? I hope so. If not, I've got the rest of the book to make you feel that way, so let's get started!

MODULE 1

Pre-Work for Success

Strategy isn't something you can nail together in slapdash fashion by sitting around a conference table.

– TERRY HALLER, author of Successful Strategist

Creating a strategy is an exciting thing. It's also an investment of your time, energy, and money.

I want this experience to be as powerful as possible for you. I want you to end up with a strategy that you implement that blows you away. In the end, revenues should increase, a competitive advantage should shine through, and you should drive sales up.

Your new and old customers will love you too.

But for this to work, we need to get a few things down. First, we'll address how to approach the project as a whole. This isn't an overnight job, so we want to prepare accordingly.

Next, you need some foundational knowledge. It isn't about "digital marketing tactics". I don't care if you know how to set up a Facebook page or an online advertising campaign or anything like that.

I do want you to know what a proper digital sales funnel looks like. There are six stages to it, and if you get it right, it's a powerful methodology to have in your business. I'll break it down for you so it's easy to remember, logically laid out, and ready to go in your business.

Enough talk, let's get down to business!

1

Preparing for Battle

Without a strategy, an organization is like a ship without a rudder, going around in circles. It's like a tramp; it has no place to go.

—JOEL ROSS AND MICHAEL KAMI,
authors of *Corporate Management in Crisis*

Introduction

Digital marketing is still new. With all the new trends, services, and concepts, it seems to be staying that way for a while.

Every social network is rolling out ad networks and introducing new features, retargeting is growing in popularity, and experts continue to pop up and endorse various tactics. Next year, or heck, next month, a slew of new experts, tactics, and networks will rise up.

So where's that leave us?

Well, with a huge burden. Ever really try to keep up with digital marketing? It's nearly impossible. If your job is to know the ins-and-outs of digital marketing *and* you love doing so, then you might be okay.

But for everyone else out there, particularly the business owners with enough going on between work and personal life, there's no chance. There's just too much clutter to always know what's valuable or a passing fad.

Don't get me wrong - us digital marketers have it tough also. We might live in this world, but that means it's our job to make sense of it all. And if you don't have a system to link all the tactics into, it becomes a huge headache.

That's why I tested out different concepts and mindsets when I approached digital marketing, leaving me with one central theory.

We only need two things: a digital sales funnel and a strategy.

We still need to invest endless hours into discovering and testing the latest tools and tactics. But when we know that the tools and tactics have to fit into a funnel and strategy, we begin to understand how the whole machine works. It's how digital marketing changes from being a business expense into a business investment.

When I discovered that I just need to focus on the funnel and strategy, I didn't *want* to stop learning. Maybe in my position I don't have a choice to stop learning each day, assuming I want to stay as an expert. But the fact that it didn't bother me anymore was a huge advantage.

Sounds simple, doesn't it?

Just two things. And you already know what a sales funnel and strategy is, right? But don't worry, we're going to get much more in-depth than that as we go through this book.

As you'll see, this book isn't about digital marketing tools and tactics. I frankly couldn't care less whether you know how to code your own website, design beautiful graphics, or run detailed analytics. I just want you to know two things: digital sales funnels and strategy.

When it comes time to get something technical done, you'll find that you can hire help to take care of those high skill, technical, and creative jobs. And if you're cash-strapped, don't worry either. I can't think of anything you'll ever need that hasn't been commoditized by the internet, making potentially extremely expensive initiatives affordable for the solopreneur.

Here's My Point

I wrote this book to help business owners and professionals develop effective digital strategies to drive marketing and sales. We forget about the non-sense trends and focus on developing a strategy unique to your business. There will never be two strategies that are alike as a result of this book.

I mentioned the two things we need and will understand from this book: a digital sales funnel and a strategy. There are two other things that are important to us, and it's the reason you invested in this: goal attainment and a return-on-investment.

I know so many out there are searching for "the best strategy" that delivers perfect results. That silver bullet...

I'm here to tell you from the start, that's wishful thinking. I'd love if I could deliver that to you. I'd be legendary, and be able to help millions improve their business. But, that doesn't exist, and never will. Everyone is just too unique for that to happen.

From here on out, it's on you.

You have to create your strategy from beginning to end. I'll give you the framework to work within and the mindset to have throughout the process, but everything from here is up to you. You need to be dedicated and eager to learn and grow.

And even though there isn't any out-of-the-box, guaranteed success strategy, I believe you can find success if you follow the method. Your first time won't be perfect, but we will focus on maximizing results, so I think you'll be happy.

In life and business, we need to ebb-and-flow with our environment, take risks, and get creative. Eventually, we end up at our destination. Fortunately, you'll have some choice over the environment, risks, and creativity. Even more important, you'll be the one to decide what your destination is.

This stuff is important.

It really is. As I consult and coach business owners and professionals, I found that people usually fall into one of three main categories:

1. Some understand the importance of digital marketing;
2. Many don't yet realize the potential of digital marketing; and
3. No one has the time to become an expert in digital marketing.

Honestly, this stuff can be daunting. But, I guess that's what keeps me busy. Like lawyers, accountants, and financial advisors, an intense focus on this specialized area is what keeps people interested in working with us.

But now, I want to show you the trick that I use to make sense of digital marketing, so that it works for you, not against you.

Before we begin, I want you to know something.

I started my agency with a mission of helping others realize their potential when they align a comprehensive strategy to their goals. Doubling revenues sounds impressive, but the real goals we have are deeper than that. Whether my client wants to travel the world, hire an assistant, or just find the time to spend with their family, I want to help them reach those personal goals. And I hope I do this for you as well.

As a new business owner, I lacked the credibility and history to prove my worth. I had a tiny budget to work with. I had to be resourceful and smart about how I got to work, or else I wouldn't be working very long… at least not for myself.

But I will tell you, by using this process and designing a strategy unique to my business, my first client came in. I spent hours networking, cold emailing and cold calling, but it was through my digital sales funnel that I got client number 1.

At the end of this book, you will:

- have a comprehensive digital marketing strategy
- understand what a complete digital sales funnel is
- patch the holes in your digital sales funnel
- understand your customers and business better
- bring more money into your business
- improve your strategic thinking

- reach your personal and professional goals
- have a framework that can be applied to marketing, business, and personal life

I can't wait for us to get started! I hope you're excited also. I firmly believe investing your time and energy into this book, and completing all the exercises, will help you to achieve each of those benefits above.

To touch on the exercises for a second, they're called "action steps", and you can download a workbook to guide you along by visiting http://PrimalDM.com/workbook/. If you don't use the workbook, make sure you at least do the actions steps along the way and keep them all filed together neatly.

And please, don't skim through the book or skip the action steps and expect to become an expert or to triple your revenues. It takes time and effort, but I'm here to help you through the process.

This is the kind of thing I wish I had when I was starting out. I think when people write about a subject like this, they all write in that way. Because when we build expertise, what's behind that is countless hours studying, experimenting, and experiencing. And it's a significant investment.

So, when we want to help others in the best way possible, we cram the best knowledge we have into a book and make it as easy as possible for our readers to succeed. And that's what I'm doing here.

And with that, let's begin…

Why do you need a strategy?

Enough with the pleasantries - let's get into it. First off, why even focus on a strategy?

That question sounds kind of awkward, doesn't it? You read it and think, *duh, strategies are important.* But do you really have one set up for your company's digital marketing? Honestly, do you have something written out, explaining the how's, what's, and why's?

Most people don't. Most people operate on the assumption that they'll start different initiatives, like social media marketing, email marketing, blogging, and so on, and eventually, it'll work out. *"It just has to catch on."*

Bullshit. You have no strategy. But we can change that now.

If you are going to invest your time and energy into something, you really need to understand *why* you are doing it. What is it that drives you? Is it really what you want to be doing?

1.1 Action Step: Let's go through a quick exercise to dig into why we're here. Just answer the following questions. I'd recommend you write this down as well.
• First, what is your business goal for the next year? • What is so important about that goal? • Why is that important? • And ultimately, what would having that do for you?

I could sit here and try to lecture you, giving you "answers". *You'll be able to hire someone to help you do the things you don't like doing each day; you can earn a little more and afford that extra vacation each year; you can get closer to systemizing your business so you don't have to work in it so much.*

But that doesn't answer why you're here. You need to answer that. And with four simple questions, I hope you just did that…

I do want to share an example from a conversation with a business owner, operating a $1.5 million business:

First, what is your business goal for the next year?

I'd like to double my sales team and break $2.5 million in annual revenues.

What is so important about that goal?

Well, I've had my eye on this place I'd like my business to be for about three years now. Having that sales team to back me would get me there.

Why is that important?

At that size, I'd have enough revenues to continue growing the business and not stress about cash flows.

And ultimately, what would having that do for you?

I know part of the reinvestment would go into hiring someone to assist me. All of the administrative work that takes up my time and some activities that distract me from what I really enjoy working on… I'd like one or two people to handle that stuff. I don't want to be the small business owner that can't be with his family without being distracted by how his company is doing.

Clarity keeps us focused on achieving our goals. Remember your "why". It'll be important throughout this project.

And don't worry if it isn't perfectly clear yet. We can be flexible with our why, but for now, we need some destination to aim for.

Building a Team

The team behind your strategy can determine whether it is successful or not. Throughout the development of your strategy, you'll learn who you need to add to the group.

For now, we are only concerned with the core members that are vital to the leadership of your business. Additionally, you may want to include someone from marketing, sales, and IT. If you are unsure now, you can always add them later on. At this stage, fewer is better.

And think outside what seems natural to you. Are your marketing and sales leaders the ones that would be most helpful on this project, or is it the social media managers and salespeople who interact with your customers all day?

Also, what about the group dynamics? You probably know better than anyone if a team will work out or not. On paper, it may sound great to have a certain set of individuals heading this project with you. However, if those individuals have a history of not getting along well, it might prove a challenge to make this work. Of course, managing group dynamics needs a book on its own.

If you aren't the leader of the organization, it'll be a good idea to keep them involved in some way. You need to determine if they want complete involvement, or occasional check-ins. Leadership buy-in is another important element that needs a book on its own, but keep it in mind.

On that note, remember that the leader of an organization sets the tide. It's important that the leader believes in a project and supports the members working on it. Without quality leadership, it can be difficult for the rest of the organization and other key individual to buy into the project.

Finally, it sounds like it would make sense to include someone in your organization that "gets" digital marketing. But, I want to warn you against that, or at least give you fair warning.

Digital marketing is a complicated beast. You can easily run into one of two individuals:

1. The marketer that mistakenly believes they understand digital marketing, but don't really know the strategy and sales funnel part (which you will soon!), or
2. The marketer that knows just enough more than others to distract us from the strategy and focus on the tactics and tools. They might overcomplicate things while trying to show their expertise as well.

Now, I don't like blanket statements, so don't rule your marketing friends out yet. But do be mindful of this risk. Don't forget about "Beginner's Mind".

1.2 Action Step: Let's make sure we get the starting team right. Write down all the individuals who come to mind you may want to include from your leadership team, marketing, sales, and IT. Now, look over that list of names. If you have any gut feelings where you just aren't sure if they should be included, cut them. Who do you have left? Any potential issues between the members? Give it a final look-over while thinking about who you can remove that can be included in the process later on. Keep the list short.

Add High Impact, Low Resource Initiatives

Academia likes to use the terms *effectiveness* and *efficiency* in a vague sense. They are important, but let's look at how they're applied in real-life.

We understand by now that there are dozens of different elements to digital marketing - enough to keep us busy for a lifetime implementing and testing each tactic. And we know that it requires an investment, including money, time, and energy.

So, we do need to focus on what the high-leverage elements are for our unique business. This is where we'll introduce a concept commonly referred to as the 80/20 rule (or the Pareto principle).

Rather than getting into the history of 80/20, let's focus on the concept for us. Simply, 20% of what we do will give us 80% of our results. In essence, it is the ultimate efficiency metric.

How does 80/20 apply to us?

- 80% of your sales come from 20% of your activities
- 80% of your revenues come from 20% of your customers
- 80% of your leads come from 20% of your marketing efforts

I'd encourage you to look at your business metrics now and identify where this applies. Look at your revenues, customers, sales team, and marketing activities. You can extend beyond that, but it gives you somewhere to start applying the principle.

It's too soon for us to use 80/20 on our strategy, but it's important for you to understand this principle. It will be vital to making sure you are both *effective* and *efficient*.

The last stage of developing your strategy will be the perfect time to apply 80/20. We will have results and measurements set up.

I know it seems early to talk about this if it will really apply at the end of the strategy development, but it's important for you to understand the concept as we go through this strategy, and as you operate your business.

Just remember, 20% of what you do gives you 80%** of **your results.

Also, when you consider 80/20, apply it to what *you* invest - money, time, and energy. What is it that you spend 20% of your time on that gives you 80% of your results?

1.3 Action Step: Time to use the 80/20 rule on your business. Think about your revenues, customers, sales members, and marketing initiatives. Where can you find that 20% of what you put in gives you 80% in return? You want to do this to learn the concept, *and* you might just discover something that helps you along the process of developing this strategy.

Understand the Risks

There is no perfect strategic decision. One always has to pay a price. One always has to balance conflicting objectives, conflicting opinions, and conflicting priorities. The best strategic decision is only an approximation – and a risk.

-PETER DRUCKER

I promise you, you *will* face risks and challenges as you create this strategy. People may push back, time and energy resources may be strained, and a sense of uncertainty will always be there. This is a tremendously important move in your business, so it makes sense. All you need to do is be aware of the risks and be prepared.

Let's take some real example.

You might need to change technologies; perhaps the platform your website is built on, or your customer relationship management (CRM) software. That means that people on your team may need to learn new technology.

It also means that people may lose or gain responsibilities, based on the changes. Again, this is why we stressed the importance of leadership buy-in early on.

How about another situation? You might need to add personnel, outsource to a vendor, or even replace the majority of someone's job.

Honestly, we just don't know at this time. In reality, none of this may happen. But the important thing is that you have this in mind, but stay confident in that you're doing the best you can for your company and its stakeholders.

And it gets personal.

There's also questioning yourself. Digital marketing is tough for many people to grasp - but don't worry. I acknowledge that, and again, we aren't talking digital marketing. We're talking strategy and sales funnels.

That said, you might see dozens of iterations on your strategy and offline and online sales funnels as we go. This is where that air of uncertainty may rise up. It happens to all of us.

Here's where your techies might come in.

Remember, smaller teams are better. With that in mind, don't think you need your technical team for the entire process. Think of them as consultants and advisors on specific questions that you have.

So why might we need our techies anyhow? Well, this is the digital space, so there's a *ton* of technologies that may help us along. The main ones to concern ourselves with are marketing automation (or Lead-to-Revenue Management) and CRM software.

CRM is something many companies will have ready for their sales teams. Marketing automation, however, is a new and rapidly growing development for marketing and sales teams.

Whichever software you look into, you have to consider three primary factors:

1. How does this fit in with the other software we use?
2. How can we transition technologically to this new software?
3. How can we seamlessly transition our people to this new software, while making it attractive to them to have to make the adjustment?

This may occur in a variety of areas, related to CRM and other software. No CRM yet? It's almost surely beneficial. Use CRM but need to upgrade your opportunities for growth? Marketing automation software might be perfect for you. How about the email marketing services you use or need?

The point is that we're just not sure exactly what you need to invest in and change now, but being mindful of different factors like this is important as you develop your business and strategy.

The key to lowering risk is the following:

- Know the basic fundamentals of how your business works today
- Consider ease of adoption when implementing a new technology, or any significant changes
- Involve your team in the process and make sure they understand the benefits if you were to invest in a new technology
- Do your research on new technologies that are available and what using them would mean for your people, processes, and current technology

There are dozens more factors that come into play when you execute a new strategy. Risk management is a tremendous subject, but when we discuss topics like this, I try to use the 80/20 principle. I focus on the 20% that you need to know to give you 80% of the results.

But please, if you're worried or want to improve your ability to lead a change fluidly in your organization, pick up another book to help you out. Remember, never stop learning.

Finally, this is an important project. It will accelerate your business forward, positively affecting every stakeholder that touches your business - employees, family, investors, suppliers, your community, and you.

Find security in knowing that you are benefiting many others by doing this, and with great potential reward, some risk is only natural.

In this chapter, you learned:

- The only two things you need: a digital sales funnel and a strategy
- Why YOU need to develop a strategy
- How to build an optimal team to support your strategy development
- How to apply the 80/20 Rule to your project and business
- The major risks that go along with developing a major project or strategy

I hope you found this introduction helpful. We covered a lot of different material, but I hope you can see *why* we got into all these different topics. They might not have precise payoffs for you now, but soon they will. They're extremely important as we go through this book.

In the next chapter, we'll take a deep dive into digital sales funnels. This is where you will understand what a complete digital sales funnel looks like and how it is used in the most successful businesses.

When we develop *your* funnel, it will be robust, comprehensive, but understandable and aligned to your strategy. That's exactly how we need it to be. After all, it is one of the main two things you need to drive growth in your business.

2

Digital Sales Funnel 101

It's not the customer's job to know what they want.

— STEVE JOBS, visionary entrepreneur

Introduction

A common issue with marketing is that it's seen as an expense. I still can't argue the "expense vs. investment" mentality when it comes to traditional advertising, like television, radio, and print ads.

However, one of the most compelling arguments in favor of digital marketing is the ability to track return-on-investment. And without ROI, it isn't worth pursuing marketing activities.

A problem still exists though. Sometimes, despite the opportunities and capabilities, digital marketing *is* still an expense. How could that be when we have so many options and analytics?

Like we said earlier in this book, digital marketing is *tough.* It's still new, and we still have a lot to learn. And even then, if we want to really "get it", we need to invest countless hours, every day. There is no time off if we want expertise.

Of course, the point of this book is that you don't have to invest all those hours. Instead, I'll break it down into the 20% that you need to know for 80% of the results.

And in the end, you're going to be far more competent in making positive digital marketing decisions and see your digital marketing strategy as an investment that will show you ROI, not an expense on your balance sheet.

The foundation to making sure our strategy does this for us is to understand the ins-and-outs to an effective digital sales funnel.

If you've ever invested dollars into digital advertising, like Google AdWords, Facebook Ads, or another form of Pay-Per-Click advertising, you'll know whether or not it worked. It usually isn't a small expenditure.

But what's really important is knowing why it did or did not work.

That comes down to the digital sales funnel.

A poorly designed digital sales funnel means a few things:

1. There's no clear path from the top of the funnel to the bottom
2. You have a tough time knowing what part of the funnel you lost the potential customers at
3. You're going to need to spend a lot to get prospects at the top of the funnel, resulting in few conversions into leads and customers throughout the funnel

We usually end up blaming other factors. Sometimes they're accurate, but often we don't even think about our sales funnel. It really becomes an afterthought.

Instead, we might blame:

- People on our team not doing their job
- Technology not supporting our marketing needs
- Digital marketing being a time-consuming expenditure, not an investment

But now we know these aren't always, or usually, the case - are they? We can try pumping more money into the funnel, test out new technology, or seek out someone who loves social media, but those are usually short-term fixes at best.

What we need to do is analyze our funnel, from top to bottom, and identify the weak points.

As you work through this chapter, you'll go through each stage of the funnel, top to bottom. You'll also get a bonus at the end of this chapter, where I give you the vital, foundational elements of the most pivotal skill I've ever learned in business. Exciting stuff!

We're all about working smart here, not hard. Low resource use, high impact. Always think *80/20.*

The best way to 80/20 your digital marketing knowledge is to understand how the digital sales funnel works. Without a funnel, your marketing knowledge is nearly useless.

You probably don't even have a digital sales funnel mapped out yet. That's okay! In fact, it might be a good thing. By the end of this chapter, you'll know each step of the funnel *and* you'll map out your own funnel. This exercise alone will pay off for the time you invested in this book so far.

Before we begin, here are the six stages of your funnel mapped out:

1. Generate Demand
2. Capture Quality Leads
3. Nurture Leads
4. Convert Leads into Customers
5. Close, Deliver, & Satisfy
6. Referrals and Follow Up

In this chapter, we will look into all six stages of the digital sales funnel. At each stage, we will look at potential opportunities and challenges. The purpose, however, is to grasp the overall concept of what makes an effective funnel, rather than the tactics that fit into each stage.

Part of our work in this chapter will be to analyze what you are doing and not doing now, while looking for areas to improve. Small steps over time can lead to tremendously beneficial changes.

Stage 1: Generate Demand

Without generating demand, we have no potential leads to move through our funnel. This is the stage we most often focus on by spending money on advertising. It's also one of the main reasons we see marketing as an expense, rather than an investment.

Generating demand, or attracting traffic to your website, is a fundamental part of an effective strategy and funnel. What's most important is that you generate demand focused on your ideal customers in an efficient way.

Later in the book, we'll get deeper into how you define your ideal customer. That's one of the most rewarding parts of this book, so I'm really looking forward to that.

But back to your funnel.

How do you define your target market now? Some ideas may be:

- Geography
- Demographics
- Common Needs and Wants
- Users of certain other products and services

It's important to make sure you're targeting the *right* market. You already know that, so we won't get into it too in-depth.

Instead, how much we generate demand using digital marketing tactics?

Here's a few ways to generate demand:

- Facebook News Feed Ads
- Retargeting / Remarketing
- Blogging and Content Creation
- Pay-Per-Click (PPC) Advertising, like Google AdWords or Bing Ads
- Search Engine Optimization (SEO), to be visible when potential customers make relevant searches on Google or Bing

Let's talk about how you decide what way to generate demand.

First, you need to develop an ideal customer profile. Again, this comes later on. In the meantime, focus on who you believe your ideal customers to be.

Second, you need to focus your energies where your ideal customers would most likely see you. *"Fish where the fish are swimming."*

For example, do your ideal customers use Facebook, LinkedIn, or Pinterest? Is it worth testing multiple channels, or are none relevant?

What about search engine optimization. Does it make sense for you to be a top listing when someone searches for *"[your product/service] in [your city or state]"*.

Again, you don't need to know the specifics of *how* to do SEO or set up an ad campaign. You just need to know what they do and if it makes sense for your situation.

When you decide what makes sense, then you want to have an employee, agency, or freelancer do the research for you to tell you how much opportunity there is, what you would need to invest, and what you can expect in return. Any skilled individual will know what information to give you if you just tell them this much.

So that's it, you're an expert at stage 1: demand generation.

2.1 Action Step: What does your demand generation look like now? Are you doing any advertising? Does your traditional advertising, like TV, radio, and print, direct potential customers to call, to visit your website, or take another action? Who are your ideal customers? Where are they online? What ways can you reach out to them based on where they go online? List all the possibilities to these questions.

Stage 2: Capture Quality Leads

The keyword here is "quality". We can get a flood of contacts, but that becomes an expensive way to waste time, money, and energy to weed out the good from the rest.

To get quality leads, you need to know your ideal customer. When you know your ideal customer, you can create offers, or "lead magnets", catered to them.

The premise is that you can offer something valuable to your website visitors in exchange for basic contact information. This is the real beginning of the relationship.

To create that offer, understand what motivates your ideal customer. Understand what they want and need at the early stage of searching for a solution to their problem.

There are three primary elements to making a great offer:

1. Always, always, always communicate the benefits
2. Make it high value to your ideal customer
3. Make it easy to receive

Advertising itself is a transaction - you receive attention, the other party receives exposure to a potential solution.

But now, that needs to continue. A good copywriter can keep attention and drive the desire of someone to continue that relationship. There's one primary element of great copy that we'll focus on now…

> **BONUS:** Copywriting is hands-down the most important skill for anyone to develop in business. So, I decided to include a crash course. You can read it in the bonus section near the end of this book. Enjoy!

Benefits

Most people have a tendency to talk about features of their offerings. It seems like it makes logical sense… We talk about the different capabilities and functions that our offerings have. Sometimes, we position these as advantages over competitors' offerings, thinking it's more effective.

To some degree, that's true. But why should we explain our offerings in an average way when we can make a simple step into a great way to communicate?

That's what we do when we talk about the <u>benefits</u>.

I like to explain my offerings using three main benefits. Here's an easy way to think about it so you don't struggle to come up with solid benefits, while also helping them to connect to different desires:

1. Financial Benefit: How can you show ROI if they become a customer? Can they increase profits, earn more money, or save on expenses?
2. Strategic Benefit: While you may not be able to calculate strategic benefit, it's still extremely powerful. This refers to the posi-

tioning of the buyer after using your product or service. It may be something that gives them a competitive advantage.

3. Personal Benefit: How will this purchase improve the quality of life of the buyer? Does it make them feel good? Does it help them avoid pain? Make it personal.

Make sense?

Use this way of thinking when you want to communicate benefits and I promise, it will help you come up with engaging ways to speak directly to what motivates your ideal customers.

Offer Value

Assuming you know who your ideal customer is, what motivates them, and what they need and want at this, early stage of seeking a solution to their problem, help them out.

What can you offer at this stage that they would find valuable?

- Infographics
- Video course
- How-To eBook
- Checklist / Guide
- Data sheets or White papers
- Free Consultation with a Specialist
- Buyers Guide for your Product/Service
- Coupons and Promotions
- Access to Private Groups

- Free Sample or Trial
- Giveaway Offering
- Webinar Access
- Product Demo

High quality is important. Make sure it's something that your visitor will want, not what you'd like them to have. For example, one of my favorites is "5 Things to Look for When Hiring Your Next [*provider*]". And you guessed it - whatever you offer as a service is what goes in the *provider* space.

It gives you a way to help them notice the red flags in your industry, while validating yourself as someone who recognizes the risks they take. Just be careful to not make it a sales pitch. Once you start to pitch yourself for the job, you lose credibility as a helpful source.

Another idea I love is the dentist who offers "The 5 Toothbrushes I Recommend, Plus the One I Use". If you're trying to take care of your dental health, don't you want to know what toothbrush your dentist uses? Also, there's the element of transparency, friendliness, and openness.

Easy to Receive

Keeping this process as low friction as possible is important to make this work.

The more you ask of your potential customer, the less likely you make it for them to decide to take that offer.

For example, nearly every new website I notice has a low-performing "Contact Us" form. What's the issue here?

The customer has to determine the value. Contacting you is only as valuable as they can conjure up in their mind. Maybe they can get value from you, but you're leaving it up to them to predict that you can educate them as they need to.

The bigger problem is the friction. You are forcing them to assume value and receive nothing but a note to wait for you to respond to them. Why would they really feel compelled to contact you in this case?

It gets worse also. Contact us forms are fundamentally stale. We'll get into that next, but let's return to making this low friction.

Consider what you are delivering to them. Do they need to commit to a two-week email course? Or can they just trade their email for a two-page eBook?

There isn't any single right answer. Sometimes the two-week email series is best - and other times you want the concise, powerful message. It's up to you to determine that for your business and with your customers.

Let's finish with building your form where you make your offer.

Now we can get back to those awful "contact us" forms…

Headlines

First, you want to grab attention in a powerful, engaging way. Your form headline does this. As a hint, "Contact Us" is *NOT* an engaging headline.

Think of the last time you held a newspaper… What did you do? We all do the same thing.

We skim over the page, and if no headlines jump out and grab our attention, we flip to the next page.

For you, that means if your headline doesn't catch attention, your visitor won't pay attention to your offer, and they might even jump over to a competitor's site instead. If they grab their attention, that's a lost potential customer.

What You Ask For

Next, what do you ask for? This is tremendously important to lower friction.

Have you ever seen a form that asked you for dozens of pieces of information? More information might empower your business by knowing more about a lead, but in reality, you end up gaining far fewer leads by asking for a lot of information.

Instead, what do you really need to give the lead magnet offer and continue the relationship? I usually recommend sticking to just name and email.

Simplicity is the ultimate sophistication.

–LEONARDO DA VINCI

The Last Step: Your Call-to-Action

On these contact us forms, they usually end with the standard, stale "submit" button.

How exciting…

Now, a button can only be so fun, right? But, there's proof in that action-oriented button text makes a tremendous difference in how likely it is for someone to click that button, initiating contact with your business.

As a rule of thumb:

- NEVER use "submit"
- ALWAYS associate the button text with what value they receive in exchange

For example, if you offer a 5-day course, your button text can be "Let's Get Started" or "I Want to Learn [X]". These are far more powerful that the standard option. You want them to think, "YES! I do want to get started," or "I do want to learn that!" Otherwise, the best you'll hear is "Yeah, I guess I'll submit this…"

These are also staples to great copywriting, referred to as "calls-to-actions", or CTAs.

Capturing leads is vital for your success.

This is when we start to fill our pipeline with potential opportunities. When you can offer someone value, you build your credibility, gain trust, and further your relationship.

That's why we want to make sure this stage is part of our funnel. Effectively capturing leads is the only way to nurture and convert quality leads into customers.

2.2 Action Step – List the three benefit types on a piece of paper: financial, strategic, and personal. Now, think of your top three for each type. When you have these nine total (you can do more if you'd like), select a single best option under each benefit type. You want the benefit that best communicates your message directly to your ideal customer.

2.3 Action Step – Review the list of potential lead magnet offers. What do you believe your ideal customer would appreciate? Can you call an ideal customer you have a good relationship with and get their opinion? List out each method, whether a video, infographic, eBook, or another option. Now, think of topics that you could cover in whatever medium you choose. It'll be best to focus on a single lead magnet for now. Later on, you can create more and test to discover which your ideal customer likes best.

2.4 Action Step – Start writing headlines you can use on your lead magnet offer. Come up with at least 10; 20 if you can manage to. You can get a list of my best headline formulas here to help you: http://PrimalDM.com/headline-formulas/. Now, what's the lifetime value of a customer for you? Notice how much you can potentially lose if you don't do this exercise to find a great headline.

2.5 Action Step – What do you *really* need to ask for? Name and email is usually enough, but if you think it's something else, just make note of it here.

2.6 Action Step – What will compel your ideal customer to take action by giving their contact information to you in exchange for your offer? Use this terminology as your call-to-action (CTA) button.

There are a lot of action steps here. I understand if it seems a little overwhelming. Rather than worrying about getting it perfect right now, focus on getting it done. Later on, you can develop your ideas further and continually improve them over time.

Stage 3: Nurture Leads

At this point, we have high quality leads connecting to us and gaining value from the offer we gave them. This is a great position to move closer to a sale.

Traditional advertising and marketing would "push" the sale on customers. For example, an email campaign asking the new lead to buy or offering discount codes if they purchase now. While that can be slightly enticing, it's more likely to be a turn-off.

If you're in a business where customers buy solely on impulse, your job might be done already. But I would guess that your customers like to take some time to consider whether or not they should buy from you. And when that's the case, you need to continue building the relationship.

We build the relationship by continuous communication with the customer. The key is that any message to our lead should be *at least one* of these three elements:

1. Educational
2. Engaging
3. Entertaining

Most messages should be educational if your market needs to learn while they are doing their research. Otherwise, you can focus on engaging content. And always try to be entertaining, over stale and corporate sounding.

Let's get clear about what we mean by educational, engaging, and entertaining. And for the sake of clarity, let's say that you deliver these messages through an autoresponder.

An autoresponder, or email nurture sequence, allows you to automate your communication with leads and customers. It would likely begin once the website visitor enters their contact information in exchange for your lead magnet, which we discussed in the previous section.

Alternatively, you can set up more advanced triggers based on links clicked within an email, certain web page visits, and other behaviors by your lead.

The key though, and why I love autoresponders, is that you can deliver the right messages at the right time in an automated way. This really maximizes the impact of your communication.

Educational

Education is important in the buying process. Everyone wants to make sure they make the right decision.

It's your job to make your lead's buying process as simple as possible. This is where you need to think about what your leads want and need to know in order to buy.

When you think educational, remember that people care more about benefits than features. While it may be worthwhile to mention features, it shouldn't be your focus.

The ultimate way to be educational is giving the lead everything they need to know to make a smart decision, and be successful with the product or service. Again, we aren't saying, "your best bet for success is to work with us!"

Instead, our messages should be more like, "if you want this to help you be successful, consider risks *A*, *B*, and *C*."

Engaging

The next two *E's* will be quicker, because there is much overlap. When we think of engagement, we want to consider how well we can connect the reader to our company.

The more involved they are in communicating with us and proactively learning about the product, the better.

For example, webinars offer high engagement. There's interaction through chat features, visually seeing someone on screen, and hearing someone speak about the benefits someone can receive when investing in that product.

And unlike in-person seminars, webinars allow you to reach an audience across the globe thanks to the digital world. But again, that's just a tactic. You want to see what fits into your strategy, so this is just an idea to clarify my point. *Be engaging.*

Entertaining

Now this is one we have to be careful with. You want to make sure you match who your audience really is.

In Business-to-Business, we often end up using highly technical jargon and dry "corporate speak", because we want to be "professional". However, that's not engaging for our readers, and it's the opposite of entertaining.

Instead, you want to think about how you would explain this as a salesman or account executive, talking to a lead in the buying process. I'm sure a skilled salesman will know how to keep things light and entertaining, without being immature or inappropriate.

Another alternative is to record yourself explaining something to a friend, then transcribe it. You're going to talk in a very natural way and explain it in words they understand. That'll give you an effective, light way of communicating your message.

And as a final note, just be careful of adding jokes in your messages. Sometimes, we end up too blinded by our pride in what we write to see that it isn't adding to our message.

The three E's give you a format for your messages, but don't forget the purpose of what you write.

Every message needs to help the potential buyer move through their research and decision phases. The nurturing stage's duration should parallel the buyer's time from starting the relationship when the lead was captured to their purchasing decision. Your offline sales funnel should give you a good idea how this tends to work.

And don't focus on selling yourself. You need to be 100% focused on:

- Your potential customer
- Their pains and problems
- The benefits of using a solution

If you do that, your nurturing stage will lead your prospects into the fifth stage: converting leads into customers.

Here are some ideas you can include on your autoresponder:

- Promotions and discounts
- Offers for free consultations
- Check-In and ask for questions
- Quick, instantly applicable tips
- A mix of long and short-form content
- Testimonials and customer highlights
- Informational, thought leadership videos
- Blog posts with highest views and engagement
- The lead magnet offer the lead first signed up for
- Case studies focusing on specific benefits or pains
- Reviews of a set of previous messages in the sequence
- Any great content you considered for a lead magnet offer

2.7 Action Step – How long should you engage your leads? It might be helpful to talk with some leading sales staff to figure out exactly how long their sales cycle is. If it's a month long, you can use that as a metric to align your nurture sequence to. Then your emails can release on the first contact, two days later, and then every four days for the remainder of the time. That would be 8 emails in the month – a decent sequence. (Aim for 5-7 emails if using an autoresponder, and always contact them more early on when the lead is hot.)

2.8 Action Step – What can you offer that would be educational to your lead? How can you be helpful to them? You might have some good ideas to carry over from your brainstorming session on lead magnet offers.

2.9 Action Step – What will compel your ideal customer to take action by giving their contact information to you in exchange for your offer? Use this terminology as your call-to-action (CTA) button.

Stage 4: Convert Leads into Customers

Now we're getting somewhere! At this point, our lead is just about ready to buy from us. They just need a little nudge to get them over the edge and sign the check.

We still need to make them ask.

I know, we said not to ask for the sale straight out before. But every great salesman knows that you need to warm up a lead first, but end with making the ask. Otherwise, a deal might be dead in the water.

Calls-to-action are how we help that lead to become a customer. The sole purpose of a CTA is to help the customer take the next step. Consider what that means for you.

For many of us, we'll assume that to be making the purchase. For you, however, perhaps the key is getting them in a product demo, setting up a consultation, or setting up a free trial.

Remember, the lead came to us, gave us their information, received instant value from our offer, and gave us permission to continue giving value as we nurtured the lead.

Now, it's time to make that lead a customer.

Focus on what the final step would be and make it as easy as possible for the lead to take that step. Like we said before, we want high value, low friction options.

Some ways to offer high value and design low friction in the process is as follows:

- Trials
- Set Up
- Training
- Guarantees (the stronger, the better)
- Social Proof (notable others who were happy to buy)
- Engaging Stories (specific to the pains, problems, and solution)

Also, you want to lay everything out in the most basic way possible. For example:

- Tell them where to click to get started
- What to do, like entering contact or credit card information
- The following action, like clicking the final CTA button, and
- What to expect next, like how long to wait for the purchase to arrive

Creativity and simplicity is usually the best way to get a conversion. Make the choices simple, with either single option, or a few that are clear on why they would choose one package over another.

And remember to always be customer-centric. This is the final step before that lead becomes a customer, and you know how important happy customers are. It costs far less to retain and upsell customers than it does to acquire new ones.

Start the relationship off right...

2.10 Action Step – What can you offer to help your lead take the final step to doing business with you? What will drive them to take the action? Map out a few possibilities here. Again, your sales team might be helpful in thinking of some of the best ways.

Stage 5: Close, Deliver, & Satisfy

This stage is pretty straightforward, but it's also incredibly important.

The Close

> *A customer is 4 times more likely to defect to a competitor if the problem is service-related than price- or product-related.*
>
> —BAIN & COMPANY

It's best to constantly improve what you are doing in business. For the close, you simply want to make sure that iteration makes the closing process easy, frictionless, and functional.

If you are taking orders online, your digital point-of-sale needs to be seamless. Simple user interfaces that appear clear and credible make the close easy for both parties.

There's a tremendous amount of psychological principles that can go into an online checkout process, but we can't get into all those here. Just focus on the concept and remember to constantly iterate.

And as a final note, your sales team will likely appreciate customer relationship management software, if they don't have any set up or optimized yet. That helps them to make sales for those of us who don't sell online.

The Delivery

70% of buying experiences are based on how the customer feels they are being treated.

—MCKINSEY

Congratulations! You've made a sale! Before we say the job's over, we got a bit more to take care of, starting with the delivery.

Since this is also highly custom to your business, the key concept is going to repeat here: make it easy, lower friction, and make sure to stay in contact with your customer. Failure to communicate is an awful way to begin a relationship.

And Satisfy

It costs 6–7 times more to acquire a new customer
than retain an existing one.

—BAIN & COMPANY

What can you do to let your customer know they're appreciated? Can you do something to show them that you're going to champion them to be their very best as a customer?

This is a great time to invite them onto your team. It goes beyond customer service and focuses on helping them feel great about their purchase.

Some ways you can deliver instant satisfaction to your new customer:

- Offer free advice on getting started
- Explain what training you offer to help them be at their best
- Show them how others similarly gained from working together

And a great way to deliver this is to add it into an autoresponder sequence, or integrate it with your CRM system so your team can reach out to them directly. Automation makes scaling your sales easier!

2.11 Action Step – Is your closing process as seamless as possible? Do you have room to remove friction and add value and credibility?

2.12 Action Step – Now, how can you ensure your delivery is seamless? Is it already as good as it can be? What can be improved?

2.13 Action Step – How can you "wow" your new customer? What would show them they're part of your family now?

Stage 6: Referrals and Follow Up

The probability of selling to an existing customer is 60 – 70%.
The probability of selling to a new prospect is 5-20%.

—MARKETING METRICS

If you don't care about the success of your customers, you're going to have a very difficult time in business. The statistics don't lie.

So now that we closed, delivered, and satisfied, we need to complete the process. One of the most effective and efficient ways to grow your business is through referrals.

Referrals

Almost any business can incorporate referrals into their sales funnel. You may mention before closing the deal that you take referrals, and perhaps that would even qualify the lead for a discount. You only want referrals *after* someone becomes a customer, so they can speak to exactly what you offer.

In whatever way makes sense for you, just try to incorporate referrals. If you keep your customers happy, they love the opportunity to help your business. Also, if they're your ideal customer, their friends are probably your ideal customer as well.

Referrals can be a powerful, lucrative sales tool that helps to sustainably automate your business. If you've taken all the steps up to this point, it should be easy to ask for a referral, and to receive one.

Here are a few ideas for including referrals in your follow up:

- Cash incentivized referrals
- Bonus feature incentivized referrals
- Giveaway drawing tickets for special prize
- Mandatory referrals for doing business together
- Exclusive access to special events or information
- Free additional time as customer (if you offer a monthly service)
- Upgrade incentivized referrals (upgrade from a mid-tier offering to top-tier)

Follow Up

Referrals shouldn't be the only follow up you do. Again, championing your customers to make them the best they can be pays dividends to you. Your customers can be your best salesmen and marketers.

Automated, periodic contact is best to do this. It can be anything value-driven, like check-ins, training, or special invitations for events or webinars.

This also is a good time to start a brand new digital sales cycle. If it makes sense to upsell or cross-sell, you can start your customer from stage 2 of this process and put them back through each stage.

This time, it will be much more successful, given your current relationship. The only risk is to be seen as a company that's *always trying to sell.* But, if you followed my advice thus far, you won't have to worry about that. Your customers should love what they hear from you, every time.

> **2.14 Action Step** – Effective referral systems keep the customer in mind. What can you offer them? What do they want most? Can you test your top two or three ideas?

> **2.15 Action Step** – How will you follow up with customers? Will someone call in every few months, or is it going to be set up as an automated email sequence? In what ways can you bring value to your customers?

In this chapter, you learned:

- How to generate demand for your digital strategy
- How to attract high quality leads based on your message and offer
- The value of a nurture sequence and how you can implement one in your business
- How to make an enticing, low friction "ask"
- Why you want to establish a seamless, valuable final stage for the close, delivery, and satisfaction of your new customer
- Why you need to incorporate referrals in your business

- How follow up sequences need to help champion your customers

2.16 Action Step – Do you know your current set up? We don't want to get lost in the details quite yet, but let's map out the full process. This will show us what stages aren't optimized, or don't even exist. You might have multiple funnels also. If so, create a separate process map for each.

If you find it helpful, you can download a PDF copy of the digital sales funnel here for your reference: http://PrimalDM.com/funnel-pdf/.

When I go to consultations with clients, I usually take a laminated copy of the funnel. They usually like to use it, since you can always write on the laminated copy and wipe it clean as needed. Try it out yourself.

In the first chapter, you learned why *you, as an individual and business,* need a strategy, what risks and opportunities go with strategy development, and how to build a supporting team to lead the initiative.

Now, we just learned how a complete digital sales funnel works. You saw how stage 1 lead into stage 2, stage 2 into stage 3, and so on. We also saw how the process can start all over again if we want to upsell or cross-sell. I promise, this alone gives you a tremendous advantage over the digital marketers out there who focus on certain mediums, like social media or email marketing!

Now, time to work on your strategy!

In the next chapter, we're going to take an in-depth look at your business, as it is today. The good, the bad, and the unknown. This is the first step we need in order to design a strategy that maximizes your opportunities and helps you reach your goals!

MODULE 2

Designing Your Strategy

Leaders establish the vision for the future and set the strategy for getting there.

—JOHN KOTTER, professor of leadership at Harvard Business School

It's time to start developing your strategy!

If you did the exercises up to this point, they're going to be very helpful in making your strategy effective and easy to understand. If not, it isn't too late to get this right the first time around.

I'll guide you through each stage of the strategy, so you can make sure you're developing something uniquely powerful for your business.

We often don't take the time to create a strategy like we will now. It's unfortunate, because a little effort upfront can result in tremendous dividends down the line.

When you have a strategy set up, it becomes easy to maintain and improve, while instantly working for you and your business.

In this module, we will look at where your business is today, where you'd like it to be, and how you can get there. I find each individual stage of this process helpful to review periodically. If this is your first time looking at your business this in-depth, you'll discover some great things.

Of course, if you're like me, you'll have your best ideas come when you least expect it - driving to the office, exercising, or in the shower. Just make sure to write those ideas down, because I think you're really going to enjoy using them after you read the next few chapters!

3

The First Step – Where are you today?

That business mission is so rarely given adequate thought is perhaps the most important single cause of business frustration.

— PETER DRUCKER, the founder of modern management

Introduction

Growth begins with an accurate assessment of where you are today.

In this chapter, we're going to begin building your strategy at stage one. This is the time to be authentic with yourself and your business. We need to know where you are today, as well as the history of your organization.

If in the last chapter you didn't do the Action Steps, now is the time to begin. We learned everything we need to up to this point. Now, we start designing our strategy.

These questions are very important – many of which I go through with my clients. Remember, there's no growth without action.

To start, I want to ask you what your role is in the business. What do you represent? What does your connection to the business mean to you? And how does this all affect your judgment of the business?

Let me explain why this is important. We have certain prejudices built into our psyche related to various aspects of our lives. If you happen to be a business owner, you will likely have a more emotional attachment to your business as it is and as it has been. That is a natural human element.

Or, let's say you're a marketing professional looking to better understand digital strategy. Consider that you may be defensive when you find you failed to notice some important aspects of creating a digital strategy. Sure, this seems obvious and you probably trust yourself not to do this. That's understandable for you as the marketer, the business owner, or whatever role you have.

I say this because I've been there. For eight years, I studied communication, psychology, emotional intelligence, and leadership development. Because of the hours I invested in these topics, I was able to be more authentic with myself. And when authentic with myself, I realized I have had times I was dishonest with myself and my failures.

Failures are only failures if we don't learn from them, though. So, let go of any anxieties you have about previously miscalculated initiatives and be happy for the lesson you learned.

Now that we're ready to consciously approach our strategy, let's begin by looking at our current sales funnel.

Your Current Funnel

In the last chapter, we talked about the six stages of the digital sales funnel. Now, we need to assess your digital sales funnel as it is. This is best done by creating a visual diagram – essentially a process map.

Generate Demand

We begin with how we generate demand. You can refer to the notes on your current advertising efforts. An important part of how you generate demand is what you lead them to do in your call-to-action...

Do they call in? Walk in? Do you call them? Do they visit your website?

Capture Quality Leads

Once you have their attention, how do you capture their contact information? Are you offering them anything of value? Are you leaving it up to them to contact you? What do you offer to ensure your leads are high quality?

Sometimes, the opportunity to give their name and email isn't even there. This is probably the worst possible thing you can do. Even if someone happens to land on your website, they won't be able to move through the rest of the funnel.

Give the lead everything they want and need to know.

Nurture Leads

The biggest part of helping them research is in the nurturing stage. You have a few options for this, like autoresponders, direct mail campaigns, or phone calls.

Are you doing anything now? How is that serving you? Have you tried other things in the past to nurture leads?

Our mantra should be in all your communications, no matter the method: educate, engage, and entertain.

Remember to make it easy for the customer to research, decide, and buy.

Convert Leads into Customers

Low friction and high potential value is key throughout the entire process. This is never truer than in the conversion stage. This is the final obstacle between lead and customer.

What do you do now for this? Do you leave it up to the customer to take the action? Do you blatantly ask for the sale? Or, do you deliver a clear message with your top benefits for new customers?

Close, Delivery, & Satisfy

Do you have technology, like a CRM, to help your sales team close deals? Do you have a digital point-of-sale? Is the delivery optimized to be a seamless process? Do your new customers love the onboarding process?

Make sure to take notes on your offline sales functions as well. They are often great resources to understand what works and doesn't work with your ideal customers.

Referrals and Follow Up

This should start simple, until we think about what we can do instead. Do you take referrals now? If you don't, why not? How can you include them in your business?

If you run into any stage where you don't have anything in place, don't worry. You're *not* the outlier (but we will make you one soon). Just make note of it and be excited for the opportunity when we fix that hole.

We're almost done — I promise.

Advertising

The top of the funnel, generating demand, is the fuel to your business - the engine that pushes it forward. There are a few things to note when you think about how it generates demand for you.

I find mindmaps are useful for analyzing topics like this, so I'll walk you through that. To explain, mindmaps are ways of organizing information in an easily consumable way.

To begin, take a piece of paper and draw a small circle with the word "Advertising" in it at the center. For each medium you advertise through, draw a line off the main circle and encompass the name of it within a circle (E.g., Magazines, TV, Radio, Pay-Per-Click Campaigns, Facebook Ads, etc…).

Now as we answer the following questions, branch lines off the mediums with the information you need to know. You can write this information on the line itself, rather than circling all of those as well.

- Where are you advertising now?
- How much of your budget goes towards each area of spend?
- Where do you see ROI?
- Where are you unable to track it to see if there is ROI?

These are things you need to know, and with some simple math, you can figure out. I'm sure you know where your money is spent, but make sure you get details on the big picture of advertising - offline and online.

Next, what message are you putting out there? Do you have one uniform statement, or do you change messages by medium, geographic location, or another key metric?

Finally, what's the action you are asking the viewer to make when they see your advertisement? Do they call in, stop by your office, or visit your website? Did you get too focused on "branding" to worry about a call-to-action?

You should have a nice visual of your current state of advertising now. Keep this on hand for step 3.

Marketing Message

We just talked about this briefly as part of advertising. We also discussed it a bit previously in the book when discussing benefits and communicating with our customers.

Coming up with a good marketing message is a tiring process. It comes as a result of a lot of time, brainstorming, and creative juices.

To get started, think about the following:

- What's your message now?
- What does your brand represent?
- How do you decide on your marketing message?

- Is your message catered to a specific ideal customer
- What do you state as your "unique selling proposition" (in other words, why you?!)?

Take a moment to think about this as it is very important. Improving your positioning in the market can be a profitable activity. To reposition yourself well, however, you need to know precisely how you *are* positioned, as well as how you *try* to position yourself.

Your marketing message should have a consistent theme throughout your all your communications (digital advertising, website copy, television, and so on).

What makes you unique should be *truly* unique. Before we get stuck thinking we're okay, let me stop you from making a common mistake... Saying that you offer *high quality service* isn't a good answer. These days, that's expected.

The best way to form your message, deciding what makes you unique and special, is to go straight to the customer. Take your *best* customers - those who you would call ideal - and call them. Ask for a short interview to help you improve your business, none of which will go to the sales team, in exchange for some small incentive. It can be as simple as a $25 gift card to Starbucks. Just do this with ten customers.

When you do this, you will also discover much more about your ideal customer. Keep detailed notes, because we're going to create an ideal customer profile very soon.

Analytics

Benchmarks give us the ability to measure change. Since we are going through a major change cycle with this strategy, we want to track and measure our progress.

If you don't have Google Analytics set up yet, just have your web developer head over to http://google.com/analytics/. Follow the instructions and you can start tracking.

Google analytics will allow you to see:

- Website traffic change over time
- What visitors do on your website
- Geographic location of your visitors
- Your most effective marketing campaigns
- What pages resonate strongest with visitors
- How much traffic comes over mobile devices
- The most valuable segments of your target market
- Which keywords work best with your ideal customers

You see, this is all valuable information. It is also valuable when you can compare months before any major changes to months after major changes, and that's what we want to do!

A quick tip on making Analytics useful after you set it up on your site, set goals.

Setting goals allows you to track specific behaviors you want visitors to take and show your progress towards that goal. For example, you can use this to see how many people work through your digital sales funnel, each step of the way.

In this chapter, you learned:

- How to evaluate your current funnel
- What advertising means for your business and strategy
- The importance of having an engaging marketing message
- Why you need to set up analytics on your site

Most business owners like this part of designing the strategy because it's helpful to work *on* their business instead of *in* their business. There's a lot of valuable insight when you do an in-depth analysis of what you are doing now.

What's really exciting, however, is when we look into the future. What's your company vision? Your goals? How are you going to reach them?

As we get into the second step - *Finding Your Ideal* - we will get into just that and help you every step of the way.

4

The Second Step – Finding Your Ideal

If a man takes no thought about what is distant, he will find sorrow near at hand. He who will not worry about what is far off will soon find something worse than worry.

— CONFUCIUS, ancient Chinese philosopher

Introduction

In the last chapter, we defined our current situation. This self-awareness prepares us as a business and marketing force to take a powerful step forward. The question is, what are we stepping towards?

When we were young, we constantly heard the same question: "What do you want to be when you grow up?" Today, it's important to ask ourselves the same thing about our business.

If you're newly in business, you might hear this a lot already. I'd also guess even if you have an answer now, within a few months it'll change. As long as you have a general idea, you're in good shape.

For our established small and medium-sized business friends, you might be clearer on this. It's expected of you to continue growing, by some standard, in some way. But what's important is by what standard *you* want to see growth.

Limiting our vision to what others expect of us, or a general metric of "growth", is harmful. It does a great disservice to ourselves, our business, and all our stakeholders. Part of our mission in business should be to drive value to all stakeholders. Having an established yet flexible vision allows us to do that.

In this chapter, we are going to dig into what your vision is for your company. From there, we will define a path to that vision by establishing goals. Finally, we will set milestones that help us on our journey to reaching our goals. This framework will help you to achieve all you want to, as long as you follow through with the strategy steps that follow.

I love this chapter, because it isn't limited to our business. We can use the same thing on a smaller scale, like if we're trying to get better at a hobby. We can also apply it to our entire personal life, setting our own vision, goals, and milestones.

So enjoy this opportunity for a deeper connection with your business, starting with who your ideal customer is.

Ideal Customer Profile

There are two parts to creating the Ideal Customer Profile (ICP): interviews and creative brainstorming and research. I always suggest interviews, although sometimes they aren't done for a number of reasons. A main reason is not knowing *how* to conduct an effective interview, so that's how we'll begin.

The Interview

If you have customers you love to work with, go to them. Like we mentioned in the previous section, you will do an interview with 10 of them. This helps you learn why they would choose you (or why they wouldn't), as well as information about how they think.

After these interviews are collected, you can compile the findings into one profile. You will likely still have to develop an outline of the avatar in a more precise way, so you should take time to read both sections below about creating an ICP.

Here's the basic structure of the interview:

1. **Priority Factors**: What drove the customer to take action relative to your service? This gets into their research stage: getting information on you, visiting your website, speaking with your sales reps, and so on. It also gets into the buy stage: What gave them the go-ahead to make the purchase?
2. **Success Factors**: What benefits did they expect when they first purchased from you? Did they receive those benefits? Do they expect different benefits now that they've worked with you?
3. **Objection Factors**: What stopped them from initially taking action? What stopped them in the process of researching, comparing, and deciding?
4. **Decision Factors**: Was there one feature that they chose you over your competition for? How about other features, how did your company stand out?
5. **Buying Factors**: What is their role? Who else is involved in this decision? What's the role of the others? What resources are considered (time, money, energy, training, implementation, and so forth)?

You want the interviewee to go back to their experience of buying from you. It's good to begin the conversation with, "Joe, take me back to the day you went to look for outsourced human resources services. What happened?"

Questions should be open-ended and get them talking. "When you decided that you needed to outsource H.R., how did you approach researching your decision? Did you ask around, search on Google, what…?"

You do want to be careful of giving potential answers to your own question, like in the above example. I might put in their mind that searching on Google was their first choice, because it makes sense to them that they'd do that. In reality, perhaps their first choice was to call a friend, but that detail was forgotten when I didn't make them think about it. Only give examples, like I did there, if they need more clarification on what you are asking.

Other questions may be, "when doing your research, what did you find, what were you unable to find, and what was difficult to find?", "what was special about the companies you looked into more?", or "what made you decide to pass on certain companies?"

The Ideal Customer Profile (ICP)

The ICP is an important element of your strategy. This is the person that you want to do business with. Hopefully you have a few customers you would call "ideal" and hopefully you already interviewed them. Now, it's time to build your ideal customer profile.

This ICP will create a single person that represents all your ideal clients. Whenever we communicate a marketing message, it will be composed directly to this single customer.

Ideal customers are those that we love to work with, but they also are the 20% of customers that account for 80% of our business. They not only happily work with us, but they advocate for our brand and bring in others through referrals and word-of-mouth.

So, that means it's clearly important for us beyond personal reasons of "who is fun to work with", but it's important for our business's success as well.

Don't be afraid to create more than one persona. Some businesses serve several different types of clients, so just one may not be enough.

There are three main parts of a profile: basic info, business info, and motivations. Have a go at it!

Alternatively, download the document online at http://PrimalDM.com/icp-download/.

Basic Info

Name		Age	
Occupation			
Lifestyle			
Income			
Demographics			
Personal Goals	What do they want, desire, or aspire to?		

Business Goals

Roles and Responsibilities	What are they in charge of or expected to manage?
Objectives and Metrics	What do they want to achieve? How do they measure success? How are they evaluated?
External Challenges	What external challenges or trends might inhibit them from reaching what they're trying to accomplish?
Strategies	What likely strategies and initiatives are in place to help achieve their objectives?
Internal Issues (B2B)	What likely issues does the organization face that could prevent or hinder them from hitting their goal?
Primary Interfaces	Who are the peers, subordinates, superiors, and outsiders with whom they frequently interact?
Status Quo	What are their status quo relevant to our solution?
Change Drivers	What would cause them to change what their currently doing?
Change Inhibitors	What would cause them to stay with the status quo, even if they're not happy with it?
What are 5 objections that this persona raises in the sales process?	1. 2. 3. 4. 5.
What are 10 common questions this persona is asking? 1.	What are your responses as an industry expert? 1.

2.	2.
3.	3.
4.	4.
5.	5.
6.	6.
7.	7.
8.	8.
9.	9.
10.	10.

Motivations

What's their biggest problem (relative to your solution)?	
What would alleviating this problem do for them?	
What are their fears, frustrations, and challenges?	
What do they like and dislike?	
What social media channels are they on?	
How do they relax?	
How do they make their decisions?	

To finish off, add a picture that represents the person well. You can use any stock photo found free online. Or, even better, if you know of a certain person that represents your ideal customer well, use that!

Your Vision

There's a chance that you already wrote down a "vision statement" for the company or the project. Even if you did, I urge you to take the time to revisit it. High growth companies in particular need an accurate vision under constant revision.

The purpose of a vision is two-fold: to point to a destination you can work towards and to give everyone involved something to hold on to during hard times.

I mentioned a vision for the company *or* project. For the purposes of developing this strategy, we need *both.* The company vision will help us understand the purpose of (and vision of) this project. It provides the foundation, as well as a better connection to our business than if we didn't consider where we want to eventually be.

So let's begin.

We tend to find it easier to use financials and metrics to say where our "ideal" is, so we can begin with that. Take a moment to list 3-7 metrics that say "success" to you and your business.

Map out two columns, listing your metrics in the first one and leaving the second empty for now. Consider all possibilities for your specific business.

Here are some ideas to get you started:

- Profit margin
- Yearly revenue
- Status in industry
- Number of employees
- Hours of your work week
- Positioning as a business
- Number of products sold

Great! Next, we have some questions to align your vision to. Don't be scared to be over-the-top here. Shoot for the stars, focus on general wishes rather than specifics that you believe you *can* achieve. Yes, you heard me right there.

- What influence do you want on your customers, your employees, the world?
- What impact should your company make?
- What's in store for the world with your company at its best?

Take a few minutes to answer these questions - list format is fine again.

Fun, right?

Now we can start to make sense of it.

Our numbers we came up with the first time give us some business-centric focus on what we want to accomplish. Now, in the second column next to each number, I want you to answer "why". What does that do for your business? If you want to go from $1m to $8m in annual revenues, what does that mean? What does it allow your business to do? And how about you? When you have your answer, ask yourself again, "why do I want that?"

For example, a spike in revenue might mean you can increase the workforce and displace some of the less-desirable tasks; and an assistant would help with that. But, is the assistant to offload work you don't want to do so you can focus on what you do best? Or, is the assistant to offload work so you can travel, spend time with family, or start a new project (or business)?

Knowing your vision is important. In this exercise, you may have to consider whether you should create two visions: one for yourself (where getting an assistant so you can travel the world is fine) and one for your company (where that same goal can be seen as lack of interest).

Make sure you took the time to go through all your metrics, ask why, and ask why again. Get it written down on paper (not on the computer, sorry). Then, we can get to the next step.

You listed your ideal influences and impacts - what are they? Who are they on? How far do you see yourself from them now? What needs to happen to make them a reality? I'm not asking for precise answers to these questions, just looking to make you think - of the possibilities, the true meaning, and your authentic desires.

Now you can form your vision statement. Write one or two sentences outlining the position your business will be in in the industry and the influence and impact it will have on the stakeholders. Be sure to balance specificity with flexibility. You don't want to say, "We will be the 3rd ranked business in our industry", but you can say, "A top 5 ranked business in the X industry".

I have to say, this is a great framework to have, but it's under constant revision, iteration after iteration. At the time of writing this sentence, I can tell you mine: "Our purpose is to provide small and medium-sized businesses with the tools necessary to attain exponential growth. With our guidance, alongside the teams we work with, we will help them achieve their milestones, goals, and vision."

I can also tell you, by the time this book is released; it's probably changed at least two times. Maybe it gets more specific, or maybe it isn't just growth-seekers we work with. But still, it's always there for me to keep me and my team strong, knowing our purpose.

And that's exactly what this does. In the hardest of times, you have your vision to look to and remember why you are doing what you do. This can be stronger than you may realize, until you are in that position.

You have a framework to find your company vision. You can use the exact same framework to find your project vision. Just go back through the steps with this project in mind, and in the end, you'll have a clearer understanding of what the project's purpose really is - especially when you can see it tied into your company vision.

Your Goals

It may first appear this project should sit in a silo with the marketing department. However, it's important to have input from every department and find out what each of them need.

It's likely best that you have each department create a matrix of "features/benefits wanted" and "rank of importance". You won't be able to make everyone happy, but with this, you can look for opportunities that a single department may not think about, as well as seeing trends in what your team wants for the business.

I'll give you an example of a matrix you can use. It shouldn't be any more complex than this, and in fact, you can simplify it. If you want to remove or adjust the "weight" and the "ranking factors", you can leave it to your teams to report 3-5 features and benefits they want, then have them rank them in approximate importance.

	Ranking Factors					
Features and Benefits	Rank each 1-5 pts.	Business Value	Complexity	Cost Savings	Time/ Energy Savings	Total
	Weight	3	1	1	2	
	Feat. A					
	Feat. B					
	Feat. C					
	Feat. D					
	Feat. E					

When you do this exercise, you want to make sure that all departments have input. This should be a company-wide initiative since it is a company-wide impacting project.

It may be for more qualified leads for sales, more ideal customers, higher revenues from online sales, more exposure, or a number of other alternatives.

Your goals need to be measurable; that is, be able to say where you are now and compare that to where you will be in the future in a definitive way. A good question to ask yourself is, "what outputs do I want from these goals?" This will help you determine how you measure success.

The final result should leave you with 1 or 2 goals to aim for with 3-5 supporting goals, also known as milestones.

The Milestones

Milestones deserve focus because they are going to be your first steps you take. You want to make sure they're in the right direction.

One aspect to keep in mind is that quick wins help adoption of the strategy across skeptical employees, which means a smoother rollout. Now, be careful not to cushion your milestones by making them easy or far off-course from what you need.

Instead, your milestones should give you enough to aim for in about six months so that it is attainable, but slightly challenging. If you have the mindset that your goals need to be extremely high so everyone strains to get there, drop it. That won't work and will likely have the opposite effect.

These should be specific as well, such as "50% monthly high quality leads in four months", as opposed to "gain more high quality leads".

The specificity will help your team work towards it, as well as your review of what worked, what didn't, and to what extent.

Also, consider the ranking factors from the goals exercise. Is there something specifically complex that you want to focus on? Maybe a milestone is implementing training so the complexity isn't a worry.

This step is highly custom-tailored to your specific situation. You need to look at what your goals are and see how you can get to them today.

One exercise to help with this is to just think of what the first step would be to move in that direction, rather than trying to think of how to accomplish the entire goal with a single milestone.

Then, think of what the second step would be if you successfully did the first one. Then the third, and so on. When you break it down into small chunks, you'll see it's far more manageable and attainable than you may initially think.

In this chapter, you learned:

- Why you need an ideal customer profile to reach your ideal customers
- How to conduct a customer interview to develop your ICP
- Step-by-step instructions to creating an ICP
- The structure of finding your ideal: vision, goals, and milestones

- How to form a vision for your business and project
- How to create great goals in your business
- What a ranking matrix can do to help your goal selection process
- How milestones can be the most vital elements of gaining adoption of your strategy

I always love to talk to people about their vision and goals and how they plan to get there. For some, they have it all planned out ready to go. Others need some coaching on how to think about it.

But "talking" and "thinking" doesn't get very much done. If you don't limit these things, they can keep you busy for hours, days, or weeks longer than they should.

Because of that, we want to start to take action as soon as possible. We have the foundation knowledge necessary to this point, so now, we need to figure out how to put it together to make us move from our current state to our ideal state.

That's what we will do in the next chapter. We will connect the dots while focusing on targeted tactics and avoiding *vanity metrics* (like the popular, misguided goal of Facebook Likes. It might sound nice, but we want to focus on reaching your goals and growing your business).

5

The Third Step – Mapping Out Your Plan

The essence of strategy is choosing what not to do.

— MICHAEL PORTER, competitive strategy authority, professor at Harvard Business School

Introduction

The third step - it's *almost* show time.

We've mentioned before that we have finite resources, specifically time, money, and energy. Because of that, we need to make the best choices based upon what we want to accomplish.

Since we established where we are and where we want to be, we have the information needed to make the best decisions for our unique case.

A major obstacle some people face at this stage is themselves.

There are two dangers we pose on ourselves: vanity metrics and poor record keeping.

We let our egos distract us from what matters when vanity metrics get involved. And inaccurate records just make our jobs more difficult and less effective.

Because of this, we are going to start this chapter by addressing both potential issues. They'll be quick breaks before we get into the big decisions. But, they're necessary breaks.

Following that section, the fun begins as we map out our growth plan.

And with that - let's start!

Beware of Vanity Metrics

Vanity metrics is more than a catchy phrase for a concept used to scare you from doing something. For many, especially young digital marketers trying to make their first projects "successful", it's a habit... an unhealthy habit.

Vanity metrics pump up your ego. They're the things you want to share with others to brag or show off. In the big picture though, they are meaningless. A popular example is how many visitors you get to your site.

"My traffic rose 300% in just the past few weeks!"
"We gained another 200 Facebook Likes over the past two weeks!"

Great, right?! I mean, it sounds wonderful.

But that doesn't translate to a growth in market share, or revenue, or improved strategic positioning. Does it really get you closer to your milestones, goals, or vision? I doubt it. There's no successful entrepreneur that's said, "I want to build a business so people can just look at it." So, why would you care if that's all your website did?

But this is the trap that vanity metrics puts us in. We end up blinded by these metrics. They're easy to see, and easy to manipulate. But the greatest things we can do for our business aren't easy.

We can end up partially addicted to checking these meaningless stats as well. It's a classic Pavlov case; classic conditioning by giving a reward instantly following a behavior. We perform an action (checking our vanity metrics), receive a reward (see an increase), and end up with that behavior reinforced, regardless of whether it's useful.

When you go to check out the latest change in stats, ask yourself "why?" Is it because the improvements signal something to you and can help you improve? Or, is it a way to kill time or get false hope?

Focus on what's important to your success.

And if it makes you feel good to check, then fine. Just be aware that it's a vanity metric, and there are other, important metrics you should check on. We'll get into those later, but for now, remember what vanity metrics are and be weary!

A Note on Good Record Keeping

"Record keeping" sounds incredibly dull. I'm sure it can be. But, it's important, and if done the right way, it can be interesting.

So what are we keeping records of? Basically, everything and anything relevant. But let's give you a template to start with. You can use any program for this, but I prefer Microsoft Excel.

In the first column, write the heading as "Marketing Activity". This simply refers to any initiative you begin. Keep it to just a title. If you want to add a note at any time, right-click on the cell and click *"Insert Comment"*.

The following column will be your metric used to track progress. For example, you might care primarily about leads generated per month, so use that. If you have multiple metrics to track, you can place one in each column. The marketing activity can correlate to only the metric column you need it to focus on, while placing an "X" in irrelevant columns as a placeholder.

Next, we want to record "financial investment". In the first column, you want to title it "Cash Outlay" or "Investment". This refers only to your initial investment for set up. Create a second column for "Monthly Costs". Again, this is something that may vary in relevance based on the marketing activity.

Now, we want to track our progress towards metrics. A common metric to follow is "Conversion Rate". It makes sense to track what marketing activities lead to conversions, whether that's calls in, appointments set, or sales made.

The final column can be titled "Revenue Generated". You can create a formula for this if you want, such as "Leads Closed * Average Sale Price". Or, you can manually update it.

I know, right now you have no numbers to enter. And, I'm going to suggest you use Google Analytics for detailed summaries of this information. However, Google Analytics can be cumbersome, and you can easily get distracted by the details.

This is something I recommend checking to focus on the things that really matter. You can update it periodically and track progress over the long-term. It's a framework, designed by you and for you. It aligns to your major goals.

Don't forget to have Google Analytics taken care of as well, but use this to periodically check in on the important metrics. Have this updated every 1-3 months.

What's working now, and what's not?

To start planning, you need to analyze what results you are getting from the marketing activities you are doing now. (You can use the template I mentioned above on record keeping.)

This is important because it helps you see the big picture of your efforts thus far. Make sure you look at your ongoing, monthly marketing spending (advertising and PR included), as well as the initial setup investments you incurred when you started these activities.

For example, maybe you implemented lead generation tactics before to your website. These are things like calls-to-actions and lead magnet offers. There was an investment to set those up, but once ready, there were no ongoing costs. You still want to take note of the initial investment.

That's why I tell clients to dig to the back of their minds and pull out everything they've ever done. As a bonus, this helps you brainstorm new ideas by rejuvenating old marketing tactics - good and bad.

List them all out, set the main metrics for each method, and calculate the return you received. Look at the good, the bad, and the ugly.

The good, the bad, the ugly - why?

If you listed out your activities from the last section, add another column on the end. This will be for "Notes". If you find any observations, quantitative or qualitative, that you think may be useful going forward, place them here. Information is power.

Even if it's from months or years ago, place that note down so you don't forget it. It just may be useful in the end.

After you do this, did you find any outliers that drove your success, or failure, that you didn't think of before? It doesn't always happen, but it could. If it does, great! Better late than never.

If you did, you also want to consider if the activity/medium, target audience, or investment made had a role in its result.

What's your competition up to?

A competitive analysis is a healthy step for any significant, new initiative. When you start to choose *what* goes into your plan, you'll likely want to revisit the analysis for the specific tactics.

For now, we want to find your notable competitors and those spending high amounts in ad spend in your industry. You should know the notable competitors. Avoid listing only those "within your reach" and include the top 3-5 in your industry. Think of those corporate giants and see what they're doing to communicate their message.

One way to measure ad spend is through a website called SpyFu (www.spyfu.com). On this website, you can enter the domain you are researching and it will tell you how much AdWords spending is used each month.

Why should you care? Well, if someone is spending a significant amount on ads in your industry, they are likely doing well with it, so you may want to see how they communicate their message and what they offer those who click on the ad. The market leaders often become experts at this.

Aside from listing the competitors and ad spend, you want to take note of specific marketing activities they engage with.

You can look for days at different marketing activities, so here are some ideas to start:

- Blogging use
- Landing pages use
- Lead magnet offers
- Google Analytics use
- Social media platforms used
- Copywriting style (words used, words not used)
- Retargeting use (Do you end up seeing more ads pop up when you go back to Facebook and other sites after visiting theirs?)

Moving from Current to Ideal: Tools, Tactics, and Techniques

It's incredibly difficult to choose a certain way of approaching the plan. There are so many tools, tactics, and techniques to choose from.

So, we're going to bring back the digital sales funnel. If you did the exercises earlier in the book, you've got a great head start on this section. If not, you're going to have to catch up. Make sure to take plenty of time to answer the questions – it's an important step to making your strategy effective.

Here are the digital sales funnel stages again:

1. Generate Demand
2. Capture Quality Leads
3. Nurture Leads
4. Convert Leads into Customers
5. Close, Deliver, & Satisfy
6. Referrals and Follow Up

Your funnel should align with your strategy. We know what our vision, goals, and milestones are, so we need to make decisions based on that.

In this section, I'm going to ask you to look at each of the first four stages of the digital sales funnel. The last two stages, "Close, Deliver & Satisfy" and "Referrals and Follow Up" need attention also, of course.

However, the exercises earlier in the book should have given you a good idea on what you can do in those stages. Instead of revising them, I'd like to focus on the content you need to design your strategy, rather than repeating material.

If you didn't do those exercises, it's definitely a good idea to go back. If you did, revisit your notes at the end of this chapter. Now that you mapped out the rest of your funnel, you may have new ideas.

Generate Demand

We don't want to get attention for "brand building" or our egos. We want attention so we can turn that attention into revenue and new customers.

In this section, we'll discuss how we can go about generating demand. It's about that initial attention from visitors who have high potential to become leads and eventually customers.

The main ways of generating demand are:

- Online Advertising
- Search Engine Optimization (SEO)
- Content Marketing
- Social Media
- Digital Communities

Each medium for reaching your audience is unique. You don't want to try them all at once, but you won't want to choose only one. Instead, focus on 2-3 mediums. An 80/20 analysis later on will show you which mediums are best, and you can always try others.

For now, I'll explain each and it should give you a good idea of what fits your business best. Always keep your ideal customers in mind. How would they most likely find you?

And remember, if at any time you get stuck on terminology, there's a glossary at the end of the book to help you out. But as usual, I try to keep this simple, direct, and understandable. The concepts are more important than the technical jargon!

Online Advertising

Advertising is the first mainstream way of generating demand. However, online advertising is a lot different than print advertising. There are countless ways for you to advertise online, but let's talk about the major few I recommend.

Before we get started here, I want to show you what an online advertising funnel should look like. I'll keep it brief, since you're already familiar with digital sales funnels.

First, we have advertisement itself. Here, we're concerned with the text/copy it uses, as well as images, if that applies. Focus on the benefits and an engaging call-to-action.

Second, we have the landing page that the advertisement links to. This is whatever web page your visitor goes to after clicking to your ad. However, you want to create one specific to that advertisement. Using a standard page, like your homepage or services page, isn't as effective or highly converting.

Finally, you have the call-to-action on your landing page. Again, we discussed these in context to your overall digital sales funnel. The purpose is to continue the relationship for further nurturing, unless it makes sense to make a sale at that point.

These three steps define a rough sales funnel. It isn't precise, but you see the approximate formula you need, regardless of the advertising channel.

Now, let's get to some of the top ways to advertise online.

AdWords/Pay-Per-Click (PPC):

PPC is targeted advertising online. The main method is with Google AdWords, which allows you to be at the top of the search engine results page when someone searches for relevant keywords that you target on Google.

I generally don't recommend getting distracted by other search engine ad networks, like Bing. Google is home to over 3.5 billion searches per day, and 67.5% of all searches on the internet. That's where you want to be.

Don't confuse this with SEO. SEO can help you to get to the top of Google with a long-term plan. For a short-term jump, PPC works. The key is long-tail, highly targeted and precise keywords.

For example, you don't want to target users searching for "HVAC services". You may want to target something more exact, like "HVAC for businesses in Springfield". That removes all the extra searches irrelevant to you, and costs much less than the more generic search term.

PPC is an intricate thing that requires continuous improvement (just like any other advertising). It's best to run a test and have someone who can fully understand the platform and how to improve what you do. If not done well, PPC can leave you with large sums of money wasted, and we don't want that.

Five Steps to a Great AdWords Campaign:

1. **Keyword Research:** You want to do deep research on 5-10 keywords. Focus on the ones most specific to what you can offer. A great way to find this is by seeing what your competitors use and the results they experience from those keywords. But don't just choose local competitors. Check on the powerhouse top 3 in your industry. They've probably figured a lot out and can cut your time to getting results fast.
2. **Campaign Architecture:** This comes down to click-through rate, landing page relevance, ad copy, and keyword relevance. Make sure the keyword, ad copy, and landing page align with each other. Make sure to improve your click-through rate over time. As a result, Google will give you a higher "quality score", resulting in better business for you.
3. **Landing Page Creation:** Don't use your homepage, or a product page. Make a page specific for that ad! It greatly improves your effectiveness, resulting in a higher quality score, and improved ROI.
4. **Bid Strategy and Budget Management:** Be careful not to use your entire budget in a few days! Set a monthly budget and make it so you gradually use the budget over the month. Make sure of this before submitting your campaign.

5. **Track and Optimize:** Measuring is the only way to improve. See what works and doesn't and keep improving. Add negative keywords, optimize ad copy, and optimize your landing page. If you don't know what this means yourself, just pass it on to whoever's taking care of AdWords. You want a specialist to see great ROI.

Facebook Advertising:

If your target audience uses Facebook, this is a great platform to invest in. With over 1 billion active users each month, there's a good chance your ideal customers happen to be there.

Facebook also offers a huge variety of options for you to advertise. Like with Google, advertising keeps revenue flowing, so they continue to iterate and improve. Try Facebook with at least a small test run. Set a monthly and daily limit on your ad spend, starting with a few hundred. This will help you see if there's opportunity for you on this platform.

Once you have an idea of what to expect, you can invest in this form of advertising and improve your ads for better results.

You can invest in this channel to increase visibility of your Facebook page, if you want. However, this is often limiting and should not be a primary factor for your strategy.

Sometimes, you want your Facebook page to serve as a "landing page" that links your visitors to a more important page. That may be a specific landing page created for Facebook followers, your main website, or a services and pricing page.

However, if your target audience would like to communicate with you over social media, create a milestone around that. Just be aware that you *need* to invest to make this happen. You can no longer rely on general Facebook use to build an audience and reach ideal customers. You *have* to pay.

But it can still be a powerful medium to use, and worth the investment. The targeting features get highly specific, including age, gender, location, and interests.

Tips for Facebook Advertising Success:

1. Use lead magnet offers.
2. Add a mix of Promoted Posts as well.
3. Focus on News Feed ads rather than cheaper, small ads on the side panel
4. Be meticulous with your targeting. Facebook has great targeting features – use them.
5. Use lots of images. Facebook only allows 20% of your ad to be text anyway. (It's a good advertising rule no matter the platform.)
6. Run a "Like" campaign only for what you need for your strategy. If Facebook is a way to communicate to prospects and customers, more is better. If it's just a landing page to lead to your website, a few hundred is plenty.

Retargeting / Remarketing:

Ever buy a new car and end up seeing it everywhere else on the road? That's what retargeting does, but with your ads.

Let's say you visit a website, doing some shopping or research, then leave and go to Facebook or another website. Then, you see the website you just left advertising everywhere. Not just after you left, but for the next few weeks, you keep seeing ads.

You're 70% more likely to go back to site and convert now. 70%. That's a huge statistic!

That's why retargeting is gaining popularity. Through multiple platforms, your ads can reappear to visitors who were once on your page. It's an excellent way of targeting hot prospects and keeping them warm.

Again, I'd recommend at least investing a few hundred to test it out. It is one of the more exciting new elements of digital marketing and should definitely be considered.

Retargeting works great for complex products and services. Impulse buys can also be pushed if you want to reignite the interest of someone recently leaving your website. Just make sure your ads appear helpful, rather than simply pushing sales.

REMEMBER…

Retargeting only reaches those who already visit your website. If you only have a few hundred visits each month, it won't be worth investing in.

However, if the numbers make sense, you have a much higher chance of converting prospects with re-targeting than any other form of advertising. It's a new favorite and popular method for a good reason.

Search Engine Optimization (SEO)

A good SEO plan is vital, but you need to make sure you are doing it *right*.

I define the "*right SEO*" in two ways:

1. Relevant to the latest trends, which change constantly thanks to Google!
2. Completely within regulations, also known as "white-hat" in the online marketing world

Please, please, please… do NOT do any SEO that may be considered "black-hat" or even the tamer "gray-hat". As you can tell by the names alone, they're steps away from the safe, reliable white-hat techniques.

These are tactics that test the boundaries (or jump right over them). If you want to have a reputable brand, it isn't worth attempting. The days are gone when you can buy a bunch of links and let that do the job for you.

Invest in an SEO specialist that understands you want to stay entirely white-hat. You don't need to know the specifics of what white-hat and black-hat are; the specialist will know. Just do things by the book.

The one thing I suggest regardless of if you plan to invest into SEO or not is *on-page optimization*. These are all the elements that affect SEO directly on your website. Find a specialist with a good reputation to take care of this for you.

Off-page SEO is a significant investment. It can be beneficial, but you need to make sure it makes sense for you. In other words, does the investment pay off by new potential leads finding you in search results?

This technique includes building backlinks (other websites linking to yours) and expanding your reach on the internet. Content creation, whether by guest blogging on another site or creating content on your own site, can be important for SEO and authority.

However, you shouldn't do things like content marketing or social media just for SEO benefits. Instead, determine the off-page strategies that make the most sense for your business. Maybe you want to attack Facebook and LinkedIn. Or maybe you want to become an authority by building a blog or podcast on your site. Decide on that first, see what impact it can have on your SEO, and then add off-page elements as you need to.

This is an extremely complex subject, so I recommend you talk with an SEO specialist to try to define a strategy. What you want to concern yourself with now is whether you believe many ideal customers would search for terms relevant to you or not.

For example, will they search, "[*your product*] in [*your city*]"? If they do, you want to appear at the top of the list when this search is made.

Here's a checklist that you can use to fix up your on-page SEO. If you're experienced, you can try this yourself. However, hiring a specialist ensures they do everything the right way, and you can focus on what you do best.

On-Page SEO Checklist:

- URL Optimized by Target Keyword
- Page Title (up to 70 characters)
- Page Description (up to 150 characters)
- Header (H1) set on page
- Subheadings (H2, H3, H4) set on page
- Image file name and alt text optimized
- Social sharing options available for visitors
- Keywords used in content on page
- Linking internally between web pages
- Sitemap created for Google and Bing
- Add site to Google Webmaster Tools

Is SEO Right For You?

If you aren't sure, consider the following:

- Do you embrace long-term strategy? (If you made it this far in the book, yes!)
- Are you on page 1 already? (While you can move even high on page 1, you want to check with an SEO specialist to see how difficult that will be)
- Do you have search volume for relevant keywords? (Determine this with a simple search test in Google's Keyword Planner tool. Another thing an SEO specialist can do for you.)

Content Marketing

Content marketing is rapidly growing in popularity. It's used interchangeably with "inbound marketing", although some argue they are different. It can also be used as part of an off-page SEO strategy.

Content marketing is exactly as it sounds: marketing with the use of content. Content can be in a variety of forms. The most popular are blog posts, videos, infographics, eBooks, and guest contributions. There are endless more options though, from podcasts to media opportunities and so on.

I'm not going to suggest a specific type of content. You need to decide on that. I want to share the concept, however. It's simple, but needs to be understood *and* remembered: content marketing focuses on sharing content with your customers they find valuable and interesting.

You don't need a "sexy industry" to make this work. This has been used for years by a variety of major brands: Ikea, Louis Vuitton, Nike, Apple, Toyota, and so on.

But it doesn't take a huge budget or brand recognition. Local small and medium-sized businesses can benefit as well; as long as they provide value to their audience.

Again, when creating content, you want to do *at least* one of three things:

1. Educate
2. Engage
3. Entertain

Content marketing isn't perfect for everyone. You need to invest the time into having your team create content, or hire an outside firm or freelancer to help you with it. As always, balance the investment with the benefit it can bring you and your ideal customers.

There is no single, perfect answer to what the best form of content is. Some people may find highly targeted traffic from podcasting, while others may have an audience that doesn't listen to podcasts.

Another might consider infographics and videos effective for visual communications, but discover it can be too expensive to outsource and take a lot of time in-house. Find what fits you.

Types of Content to Consider:

- Podcasts
- Blog Posts
- Guest Blog Posts
- Infographics
- eBooks
- Guides
- Videos
- Lists
- Case Studies
- White Papers
- Resource Compilations
- SlideShare Presentations
- Reviews (Books, Products, Events, etc.)

Social Media

Social media *can* be a powerful tool, but it isn't for everyone. There are a couple of things to consider when thinking about engaging with social media.

Answer the following:

- Do I have the resources to dedicate to this? (Time, energy, money)
- Is it worth investing resources into social media? (Opportunity cost)
- What budget can I set on this and do I need to set on this to make it worthwhile?
- What networks are my ideal customers on?

You can use one of two strategies with social media:

1. Use it as a "landing page"
2. Invest time, money, and energy into it

Social Media as a Landing Page

For many businesses, including my own, I recommend thinking of social media as a landing page.

What I mean is that you want to have a page on a major network like Facebook or LinkedIn, but that doesn't mean you need to invest heavily into marketing on these channels.

Instead, you optimize the profiles so anyone visiting understands the benefits you can offer and are then linked to another source that they can continue researching on - likely your homepage or a specific landing page.

Meanwhile, to make it clear you are still active and in business, post a few times a week, just 3-4 times should be enough. The posts can be scheduled with a tool like Hootsuite and the content can be curated from other sources.

If you do this once a month, it will only take someone about two hours of their time to ensure that your Facebook page shows you are still an active company.

Investing in Social Media

For others, you may want to engage actively on social media. If that's the case, just revisit my questions before to plan it out. Where are your customers? What can you invest? What do you *need* to invest?

Remember, to build your reach you may have to invest in advertising. Facebook specifically almost mandates advertising for you to grow your reach. You don't need to invest a significant amount, but again, think opportunity cost…

But okay, that isn't for everyone either. Maybe social makes sense for you. The first decision to make, then, is what social network to join?

To start, you should be using analytics to track what you have set up now. If you're already deep into a social media campaign over Facebook, Twitter, Instagram, and LinkedIn, see what channel(s) leads to more conversions for you. Do people click over to your links on Facebook or LinkedIn more? Is there 20% of your social media efforts that leads to 80% of your results? That's one way to focus.

But let's also break each down by target, communication method, and business types. This should serve as a guide to you to select one of the best channels for your business.

Facebook:

Target: Nearly anyone. Facebook ads allow you to focus on highly specific niches. You just want to be sure your target market is on Facebook. These days, almost everyone from teens to grandma and grandpa are on Facebook. Instead, measure whether this is the network your target is most on, or one of the others we will mention in a moment.

Method: Be personal. Have a personality. Ask questions. This isn't the place to push sales (don't make offers more than once a week, by the way). This is about building a brand, reputation, and connection.

Business Type: B2C products and services.

Twitter:

Target: Younger crowd. Focused on men and women in their twenties. This is a hard-and-fast type of network with many short messages. Noise is high, but you can stick out.

Method: Remember, 140 characters is not a lot. Beyond that, you want to make it short enough that people can quote you and respond to you with your message. The best is to shoot for 70 character messages. Make them interesting and interactive and you have something going here.

Business Type: B2C products and services; B2B unless you are in a complex-sales situation.

LinkedIn:

Target: Business professionals - simple as that. People are on LinkedIn to connect with peers, make deals, or find a job. Keep that in mind in your messages.

Method: Your messages should help them to connect with others and learn new skills. Beyond that, if you can become a connector that introduces people to each other, you'll do even better.

Business Type: B2B!

Pinterest:

Target: Middle-aged women, moms, and teen girls. 70% of users on Pinterest are women, which is great if that fits your target market.

Method: Pinterest is built on shareable es. Make sure all your pins and collections are vibrant. The images should jump out and grab attention. Mix in pictures relevant to your business and industry with pictures that hit common hobbies and interests of your target audience. It mixes things up and builds connections.

Business Type: B2C!

Again, this is a guide, not an absolute command. There are also plenty of other social networks out there to consider.

Always experiment to see what works best for you. New social networks aren't out of the question either. If it fits your audience, the new, up-and-coming networks the mainstream doesn't know about may be the best way for you to invest your time. It's up to you to experiment and figure that out.

Digital Communities

You should always "go where your target customers are". I'm sure you're familiar with that concept.

The internet gives you infinite further possibility to directly engage your ideal customers where they hang out online. Social media, message boards, niche forums, self-hosted platforms... The opportunities are endless.

The important thing is to schedule some time to focus these efforts to find where your target audience is and what to communicate to them.

When you do find them, avoid coming off as "sales-y" and pushing your offerings on them. Remember the three E's you use in content marketing. Just share information and answer questions. *Be helpful.* This is a great way to use content marketing to communicate your authority and ability without being sales-y.

You can still post your content that is hosted on your website, but use a question that everyone wants answered (and that you content answers) in the headline, share it, and be available in the conversation around it.

Some Places to Find Your Customers:

- Facebook groups
- Message boards and forums
- Reddit pages

- LinkedIn Groups
- Quora
- Major and Niche Blogs

Being Ready for Demand

As a final note on generating demand, you also want to make sure that visitors won't "bounce" off your page once they get to it. There are two driving factors that cause this: slow page speed and lack of mobile-responsiveness.

Mobile-Responsiveness

I would never even work on a project where the website is not mobile-ready. The design is the primary piece that needs to be easily viewable on a cell phone or tablet. However, you also need to consider how images appear and scale correctly.

With 80%+ traffic coming by mobile devices, you need to be ready, or else the traffic you do attract may just vanish.

Page Speed

Ever go to a website you wanted to visit, yet after a few seconds of loading more than you feel like, you just quit?

Your prospects can do that too if your pages load too slow:

40% of people abandon a website that takes more than 3 seconds to load.
47% of consumers expect a web page to load in 2 seconds or less.

That gives you so few seconds to keep your prospects on your site. It's a commonly overlooked but incredibly important metric to improve.

Run some page speed tests at the websites below and pass it onto your website developer to look into the issues:

- PageSpeed Insights (https://developers.google.com/speed/pagespeed/insights/)
- Pingdom Website Speed Test (http://tools.pingdom.com)
- GTmetrix Performance Analysis (http://gtmetrix.com)

Capture Quality Leads

Now that we have attention from potential customers, we can start having some fun. To move forward, we need to capture contact information of these potential customers. This gives us permission to continue the conversation beyond their initial contact with us.

Start with a Strong Headline

Copywriting is an art form. One of the leading elements of copywriting is headlines.

Headlines are what catch our attention, draw us in, and make us want to read more. I want you to understand the concept that the headline is the most important piece of copy you can write, because it is the passage that brings the reader to the rest of your copy.

And it isn't so much that the headline is most important. The real rule of copy is this:

Every sentence should make the reader want to continue on. The headline should make them want to read the subheading. The subheading should make them want to read the first line of copy. The first line should make them want to read the second line. And so on…

Here's an example we can all understand… Think of the last time you picked up a newspaper. You had the front page open, skimmed over the headlines, and if something caught your attention, you read further. If not, you flipped over to the next page.

On your website, that means if no headlines are catching attention, the visitor will flip over to the next page, which is likely back to Google to look at one of your competitors instead.

So, create powerful headlines. Here's a few ideas on how to do that well (always being aware of your ideal customer's mindset):

- Speak to benefits
- Target pain points

- Ask a must-know question
- Make it slightly mysterious (but not misleading)
- Use lists, cause everyone loves them (top 5, 10, 23, etc…)

Asking for the Information

Unfortunately, many businesses have fallen into the trap of relying on the visitor to take the initiative to find a "Contact Us" form and fill it out (including the unnecessary information requested).

This doesn't work. You may see a few prospects come in through this, but in reality, your visitors are doing research. That probably means they aren't looking at just you, but also your competitors. How are you going to make sure you stand out from the rest?

At this stage, we know there is some interest in what we offer. We know the prospect is hunting to cure their pain, and we may offer a solution for them. We need to show the prospect that this potential exists.

We've talked about this in-depth in the previous chapter when we discussed the second stage of the funnel. Now it's your job to create a compelling offer and design a form that is simple, direct, and to the point.

Ask for only what you need and offer something great in return for it. Lower friction, increase potential reward.

Homepage, every page, or Landing Page?

Now, we have a few options on *where* to place the form for visitors to complete. The homepage should almost always include a form in some way. It can be a pop-up or slide-in style, or a static form that stays on the page.

Alternatively, and much better but more resource intensive as well, you can create specific forms for each page. This will allow you to cater the form to the prospect's specific interests, based on the page visited.

For example, some companies have several divisions or product types that differ from one another. Using separate forms can tailor the form (and headline) to that prospect's interest, and it can send the lead to the best-fit salesman.

Finally, let's talk landing pages. A landing page technically is any page that a visitor can arrive at or "land on".

In practical use, however, there are a few fundamentals to landing pages:

- Specific target market focused on
- Specific source leading to it (like a certain AdWords ad)
- Focus on one conversion type, usually to complete a form
- Remove all distractions, including navigation to the rest of your site

For example, you may be a full-service advertising agency, but want to push your media buying offerings. The landing page can be used for visitors who find out that you offer media buying and want to learn more through another web page or an advertisement.

Now, rather than being distracted by dozens of options on a normal web page, the landing page removes the navigation and focuses all attention on getting more information about media buying.

Landing pages are most effective if you are looking to convert more leads. Each landing page will take time to develop, but they are a small investment for what they allow you to do, *if* you invest in them wisely. Using landing pages as opposed to your home page or a product page increases conversion, and ROI, tremendously.

What to Offer?

To convert visitors into quality leads, we want to offer something they need in their journey as a buyer seeking a solution. At an early stage, it may be a financially-driven educational incentive, like a free quote, pricing sheet, or 15-minute consultation.

At a later stage of their buying journey, they may prefer proof of what you offer, its benefits, and results of previous customers. Case studies or a small eBook may be a good way to offer this.

Your options of what to offer are virtually limitless. You should test different offers and see what converts the best. Just be sure that before they receive the offer, you receive their contact information.

For example, if they get a free consultation by phone, you need to get their phone when they call you, or they need to enter their phone in a form online and that gives you information to follow-up with.

The same is true if you offer a download, like an eBook or pricing sheet. In exchange for the download, you get their information.

That reminds us of another important point: make sure the information you ask for is kept to a minimum. It is easy to ask for more than you need and get lower responses as a result. Name and email is probably the maximum that you really *need*. (Although you may not need the name, it's usually best so you can personalize future messages.)

Here are a few potential offers you may use:

- eBook
- White Paper
- Pricing Sheet
- Infographic
- Consultation
- Demo
- Free Trial
- Pricing Quote
- Online Course (by video or email)
- Discount/Promotion

And here are the keys to getting the offer right:

- Offer something your ideal customer wants and needs in their buying process
- Make it high value, low risk, and free

- Ask for the minimum of what you need in exchange to lower friction
- Make the offer stand out - don't let it get lost on the page

If you follow these simple guidelines, you should see a tremendous boost in responses compared to your original "contact us" form.

Nurture Leads

Now that we have the client's contact information and the foundation of our relationship built, we need to continue the communication to move the prospect through our digital sales funnel.

There are two primary and similar ways of doing this:

1. Email Newsletters
2. Autoresponders

Email Newsletters

Many businesses already participate in "email marketing". Most send out a newsletter each week, month, or quarter. Others randomly send out email blasts whenever someone in the organization decides to. Unfortunately, it's often too often, too sporadic, or too random.

I bring up email newsletters as a less sophisticated alternative to autoresponders. Essentially, autoresponders are just another form of email marketing, but the distinction I make is that generic email newsletters consists of email blasts set to some schedule (E.g., monthly newsletters).

Newsletters have their place in marketing. They are great to broadcast educational information, keep your brand relevant, and share your clients' successes.

They are awful for you to push your services. They are awful if they are not easily read and digested by viewers. They are likely awful if you try to design and style them!

Here's some basic guidelines to help you use effective newsletters:

- Set a schedule and be consistent
- Remember your copywriting basics
- Use few-to-no style and design elements
- Be personal and make the newsletter personal
- Share your clients' successes, but don't shift the focus to how you did it
- Only send information that is educational, engaging, and/or entertaining

Autoresponders

Autoresponders act exactly as the name sounds: they automatically respond to a customer with a sequence of emails tailored to their interests and needs.

I believe autoresponders to be the best form of email marketing. After you initially set up the sequence, subscribers will automatically receive the emails to nurture them from warm leads into hot prospect, ready to buy!

But, there is some upfront work needed to build an effective email sequence. And still, once it is created, it is always best to continually revise and improve upon the emails.

To create your autoresponder, consider the following:

- How long is your sales funnel? (Match your autoresponder to this.)
- How often should you contact them? (Aim for every 2-3 days early on and up to a week in between emails later in the sequence.)
- How many emails should I send? (5-7 is best in most cases. Some may want fewer, while others can go on for dozens of emails. Think about your customer.)

What should you include?

- Educational, engaging, and entertaining content.
- What questions are you frequently asked? Answer those.
- Do you blog? Those topics can be pulled out and used or linked to.
- Any case studies ready to go? They're a great way to build trust and prove what you can offer

If you aren't yet, take advantage of autoresponders! Start building one. It is an excellent way to improve, streamline, and automate your marketing and sales process.

And over time, you can build out more autoresponders that are tailored to specific audiences and situations, so you know you are doing the best job possible to nurture each lead into becoming a customer.

Convert Leads into Customers

Business owners love the conversion stage. This is where we begin seeing revenue flow in!

At the convert stage, you take your leads that have been nurtured into educated, interested hot prospects and give them the last, small push towards being a customer.

There are a few different elements that characterize this stage, including:

- Sales pages
- Calls-to-action
- Guarantees
- Testimonials
- Case studies
- CRM integration

Sales Pages

When you hear "sales page", think of landing pages. The difference is that sales pages have a single purpose: make a sale. The call-to-action, therefore, is to buy.

This is the frame that you will build upon as you read the rest below. Powerful CTAs, guarantees, testimonials, and so on all have to be integrated into your sales page. That's how you make them powerful.

Calls-to-Action (CTAs)

The purpose of a CTA is to compel the viewer to take an action.

You want your CTAs to be powerful by engaging the prospect in a way that makes most sense for them. In other words, your CTA has to flow in the message that it appears in, be a logical and clear next step, and offer something of value to the prospect.

When crafting a CTA, there are a few guidelines you want to keep in mind:

- Concise and to the point is often best
- Make the CTA flow with the rest of your message
- Make the CTA also stand out visually from the page
- Always be action-oriented ("Submit" and "Contact Us" doesn't count)
- Speak to the prospect's emotional wants and needs, given the situation
- If the CTA is working off another page, like from an ad, match the text

Guarantees

If you can make a strong guarantee, do so. More often than not you can.

Guarantees are ways for you to say, "I'm confident you will get the results we promise." It isn't a way for you to lose money, so erase that fear in your mind.

Companies selling products for thousands of dollars use guarantees all the time. I remember a company that wanted to do better than a full money back guarantee. Instead, they offered double the customer's money back. And, that product was for a few thousand dollars.

The result of these seemingly over-the-top guarantees are simple. You see sales climb, and few if any increase in guarantee redemptions.

It seems the more audacious you are, the more comfortable the customer feels. And when you do offer to put money back in their pocket, like the double money back offer, they seem to grow wearier of asking for that guarantee. But, I haven't tested that!

However you look at it, as long as you offer a quality product or service, a strong guarantee will pay itself off with new sales. These sales wouldn't otherwise happen, so don't deny the power of a well-formed guarantee. Now, think about what you can offer.

Testimonials

If there is one thing about the general population that is consistent in their buying journey, they don't like to be early movers.

Now, there are certain individuals who want to be the first one to purchase. It's the 5% that want the latest and greatest technology. These are the people who are the first to buy products like Google Glass and smart watches, or the equivalent in your industry.

While that can be an important segment for you if you have those types of customers, the majority won't be like that. It's great for new product introductions, but not for sustainability.

The majority of your buyers *will* be risk-averse and need some reassurance.

But to this point, *you've* only been telling your prospects about all you can offer. But they know your motive – you want to make a sale.

But they can trust others outside your organization – your customers.

So use that to your advantage. Get a few customers to give you testimonials. Most of the time, your happy customers won't even need convincing in any way. If you want, you can still give them something like a $25 gift card to Starbucks as a token of appreciation.

A few keys to great testimonials:

- Concise is better than lengthy
- Speak to specific pains, solutions, and benefits rather than generalities
- Include a picture of the customer for use on website and print materials
- Link to the customer's website or LinkedIn page (Twitter is another option; Facebook

can be too personal. Remember, you don't control what they publish online.)

Case Studies:

Think "testimonials on steroids" when you hear case studies.

The purpose is to offer an extended outline of a successful project you have worked on with a customer.

I believe you should always have at least one case study available (one case per service or main benefit would be even better). If you feel that they work for you and you want to create a dozen, go for it.

But make them impactful.

Here are a few steps to creating impactful case studies:

#1 - Pick the right clients

- Who have you helped significantly with a specific problem or challenge?

#2 - Ask the Right Questions*

- What was the challenge your company solved?
- Why was it a challenge?
- What was your process for solving this challenge?
- What did you have to do that was different from the typical jobs / projects you do on a day-to-day basis?
- What was the result?

- Why is the result significant? (The "so what?")

  ** Note, these are answered by you in the client's perspective. If you want to interview the client to get the message in their words, you can do that as well. It's more preference than anything.*

#3 – Write the Case Study

- Use the "Challenge, Solution, Result" framework to structure the case
- Use bullet points for main ideas (and other copywriting principles)
- Be specific over general. Specificity = Believability
- Be concise, clear, and helpful to the reader

#4 – Finalize the Case Study

- Create a one-page PDF version (longer is possible, but 1-2 pages is often enough
- Include a photo, if possible
- Add a CTA early on and at the end (what do you want the reader to do next?)
- Include your company logo and contact info
- Double-check for errors
- Put into use (in the hands of your sales team, on your website, in your marketing, etc.)

Case studies don't have to be difficult, as long as you have a format to them. Use this as the framework to help you create your first one.

CRM Integration

As a final note, make sure that you integrate your CRM (customer relationship management) system with your online activities. That means when someone fills out a form or joins your email list, you want them included on your CRM as well.

It shouldn't be difficult for your team to figure out how to do this. All it takes is a simple Google search ("[My CRM System] [what I'm trying to do]") or a call to your CRM provider.

If you run into a situation where there's some trouble making your CRM and other technologies work together, try visiting Zapier (http://zapier.com).

Zapier is a great service that integrates different apps and technologies together. It can also be useful to automate some events. So, whether you have a problem connecting apps or not, it might be useful to spend 15-minutes on Zapier to see how it might be helpful to your business processes.

And finally, don't forget to incorporate your CRM into your email marketing service. If you use popular software, there is likely a smooth way to integrate them together already. Check with each provider and figure that out. If not, Zapier may be useful again!

A Final Note

Remember, the relationship doesn't end when the prospect is converted. Earlier in the book, we discussed the entire sales funnel. Each segment is vital to your business. These are just the four I wanted to touch on that businesses most often need to focus on, yet consider to be their most developed areas.

In the end, you still need things like social media, referrals, and content marketing to continue growing your business, even when a prospect turns into a customer.

In this chapter, you learned:

- What vanity metrics are and why you need to avoid them
- What good record keeping looks like and its importance
- How to evaluate your current marketing
- How to generate demand through Online Advertising, SEO, Content Marketing, Social Media, and Community Groups
- How to capture leads with strong headlines, asking for the right information, using landing pages, and making valuable offers
- How to nurture leads with email newsletters and autoresponders
- How to convert leads into customers with sales pages, calls to action, guarantees, testimonials, case studies, and CRM integration

This was an exhausting chapter! You have a lot to consider, and that's why it's so important that you create a strategy rather than trying different tactics randomly.

Remember to look at your funnel as it is now, spot the weak areas, and look to improve and innovate. Don't fall victim to doing the same things you did traditionally, only different. Mix in improvements with brand new initiatives.

When you've made your decision of different ways to attack your problems, you can move on to the next chapter. This chapter will guide you towards implementing the strategy and making it work for you.

One of the big things we'll get into is measuring your success. We already got started by starting our good record keeping document early in this chapter. You did that, *right?!*

Now, we can get started on your campaign and get closer to reaching your vision and that ideal, future state for your business.

6

The Fourth Step – Getting Your Hands Dirty

Success doesn't necessarily come from break-through innovation but from flawless execution. A great strategy alone won't win a game or a battle; the win comes from basic blocking and tackling.

— NAVEEN JAIN, entrepreneur

Introduction

At this point of the book you might be thinking *"FINALLY"!*

I get that. But unfortunately, there's a lot of groundwork to cover early on. Marketing is primarily done before the campaign is even started.

But don't worry - we're finally at that point! The campaign is going to begin.

In this chapter, we are going to look at the plan you put in place and see what we need to learn, do, and invest in to make it happen.

Beyond that, we need to also make sure to measure and monitor everything we are doing. This isn't only for quality assurance, but to make future campaigns even more impactful.

And of course, there will be the moment you've been waiting for. The time to pull the trigger, putting all this information you gathered and decisions you made into action.

I hope you've been taking action up to this point. It is really much more impactful if you work along with this book than try to read through it and just "see" the value.

Taking action allows you to realize the power of a well thought-out strategy.

So please, build your ideal customer profile, evaluate your current digital sales funnel, and prepare your team to do something great…

What do you need to learn and invest in?

Now you might want to just get started - throw together an advertising campaign and let it run its course. It's tempting and there's anticipation, but we can't do it that way. Not if we want to be successful, and especially not after all the work we did this far!

We need just a few more things before we execute the strategy.

And the first one is being clear on what we need to be capable of to get this done. What may we not be prepared for quite yet...

For example, perhaps your digital funnel could use technological assistance from a CRM system or marketing automation. Does anyone on your team know how to implement and manage these systems, or do they need some time to learn? Or, will outside assistance and training be worthwhile?

Let's try assuming you are investing in Google AdWords ads. Do you have someone in-house that knows how to set this up? Do they know how to do quality keyword research? Can they manage your bids and budget well? And who can back this all up with a quality landing page?

You see, there's a lot to these projects. That's why it's tough to put the execution of your ideas on just one or two individuals. Consider outside help, or training to help your team be ready to get the work done *the right way*.

Don't push away from a certain technique if it requires additional learning. Just make sure your investment in your team or another firm makes sense for your goals.

Let's also consider the project risks that go along with these investments. Remember, your staff may be resistant to having to learn new technology.

Also, new technology might mean more (or less) manpower is needed. Does your staffing align with this new technology and the new initiatives?

Don't get stuck in preparation mode, but don't get stuck in a painful situation either. Look ahead and plan as needed.

Numbers: Moving You from A-to-Z

Time to bring back out your records we started in the last chapter. It's time to build onto what we have.

You want to think, "What will move me from my current state to my ideal state?"

- Is there a certain number of sales needed?
- A certain increase in revenue?
- Do you need a higher conversion rate or increased traffic?

If you have been keeping good records, you might already know your conversion rates and traffic numbers.

If not, it may be easier for you to determine revenue and sales goals.

Whatever you choose, make sure to add the columns necessary to your spreadsheet to track your progress towards these objectives.

This may be an important aspect to have input from your entire team, as well as sharing the result with your team. Salespeople and marketers need to know what goals they are working towards.

The Big Moment: Starting your campaign…

Yes, I'm serious. We are getting started!

Enough information gathering and decision making. Time to take action.

Let's put all our energy and effort into use and get this campaign started!

The framework for this stage is simple:

- Outline all your different marketing methods chosen
- Decide on a prioritization order
- Assign responsibility for each area
- Set deadlines for each area
- Get to work and start implementing
- Test, Test, Test!

I can't say the final point enough: test what you implement!

Launches are exhausting and exciting. You can't let either of those aspects drive you away from testing.

I've made the mistake myself at times. Something as simple as shooting out an email broadcast can go wrong if you don't test.

Maybe it won't seem like a major hiccup.

But what if that email would have gained you just one more client? Mattering on your business, thousands of dollars might be lost from a single, small error.

So please, take the time to test.

Regular Monitoring

There are a few tools I recommend to monitor and measure your successes.

Analytics

Google Analytics is the most popular way to track activity on your website. It is pretty basic to set up and will help you determine how many visits you receive and some basic demographics about those visitors.

Anyhow, tracking specific elements of your website and marketing campaign as well as regular updates is important. You'll want the more advanced insights, so consider hiring help. You'll want to outsource the work to an expert.

Knowing all the information possible about your visitors can really help you better align your messages and improve the user experience on your website.

Remember, it isn't just about traffic and page views. Advanced insights can make a big difference in your business.

You could look for someone to join your staff, but it isn't economical and is limiting. You don't need someone full-time. If you add it to someone else's job or lump all website or marketing tasks into a single job, they will be a "master of none". You don't deserve that, and neither do they.

Here are some ways you can use analytics:

- Cross-reference most visited pages with the duration of a visit to see the pages that really matter
- Set goals for a certain web page being visited, such as a "Thank You!" confirmation page
- Set a goal for "Pages per Session", so you know when you have higher-engagement with visitors (E.g., they visit at least 5 pages)
- Set a goal for duration to find confusing elements – should someone really spend 10 minutes on your "getting started" page, or does that mean its difficult for them to follow?
- Set UTM parameters to know *exactly* what's working, and what's not

UTM parameters? Okay, let's touch on that for a second. UTM parameters are connected with Google Analytics, giving you and the system a way to clearly track individual sources. Simply, they're tags on your links.

A URL with UTM parameters would look as follows:

http://primaldm.com/ebook?utm_source=book&utm_medium=clickthrough&utm_campaign=strategy.

You can use Google Analytics URL Builder to get this done for you easily.

Ways to Use UTM Parameters:

- In email newsletter campaigns
- On social media posts
- Through your email signature
- Via your online advertising platforms

Tracking Traffic Sources

The flow of visitors at the top of the funnel is the only way to eventually land some customers. So, it clearly makes sense to keep tabs on the top of the funnel.

For every hundred visitors, 1-2% may turn into a lead. It can be more, or certainly less, but this is a typical number to guess on average websites. After completing the strategy, you should see this climb slightly - but don't expect double digit conversions on all visitors.

Knowing *where* visitors come from and *at what rate* they convert from these sources is helpful to 80/20 your strategy. What is really driving quality traffic?

Content Engagement

How effective is the content you create? Well, we can track that, too!

There's a few ways to find this in Google Analytics. My favorite are:

- Pages per Session
- Average Session Duration
- Bounce Rate (Lower is better as this refers to how many quickly visit then leave)

Again, this will help you figure out what is working and what is not.

Email Marketing Analytics

Any decent email marketing platform will give you the basic analytics needed to see what campaigns are working, and what are lacking. These include the following:

- Open Rate: What percentage *open* the email. Aim for 30% or higher.
- Click Rate: What percentage *click* a link in the email. Aim for 4-5% or higher.
- Click-to-Open Rate: Simply, (# of clicks / # of opens). This focuses on the clicks of those who actually *saw* the links, for more accurate reporting. Aim for 20% or higher.

Heatmaps

Heatmaps are creative tools that help you to see how your visitors interact with your page.

They help you to see how the mouse travels over your website, and what popular areas are noticed and clicked on.

It's the difference of having to guess at why visitors are attracted to certain elements of your website and knowing exactly what drags them from one spot to the next.

Here are a few popular tools I'd recommend:

- Crazy Egg - The long-time kind of heatmapping technology
- SumoMe - A more recent entrant to plugins. SumoMe offers a dozen great apps on their plugin, one of which being heatmaps. And, it's incredibly affordable.
- Inspectlet - These guys went beyond heatmapping to show you the exact user experience. It isn't just a heatmap, but a recording of user experiences.

When you see heatmaps, you can see trends that occur. You can see what is working, and what's not.

You may even notice a trend commonly referred to as the "F-Layout". This is the natural, common way we scan webpages: starting at the top-left we scan over to the right, then we go back to the left side under where we started scanning over about 67% of the page, then we return to the left and scan down the rest of the page.

The eye-scanning is essentially shaped like an "F" – and so we have the "F-Layout".

That's just a little extra information for you. Next time it's time to redesign your site, make sure your designer considers the F-Layout.

Records

Again, remember to keep your records up to date. You want to track the traffic generated *and* conversions made from all your marketing tactics. Google Analytics will be a tremendous help for this. Your own tracking sheet is limited to the major metrics, but the details are important for smaller, ongoing improvements.

Schedule regular updates, whether weekly, biweekly, or monthly, so you can keep your records updated and accurate.

In this chapter, you learned:

- How to evaluate if you're ready to take action
- What numbers you need to aim for
- What tracking/records you need to keep as you move towards those numbers
- How to use analytics, heatmaps, and records to monitor your progress

Implementation is your time to shine, but do it the right way. Please, go through this chapter and be sure that you implement your strategy the *right* way.

Poor implementation can ruin the best of strategies.

And aside from warning you from poorly executed strategy, I also want to warn you about *inaction*.

The only way for a strategy to work is to take action. Basic, simple stuff - I know! But, too many times people will read a book or go through a program but not apply the material.

This book is worthless if you don't apply what you learn - whether it's from the past sections or this implementation phase.

Don't let this book be worthless - take action!

> *The greatest strategy is doomed if it's implemented badly.*
>
> —BERMARD REIMANN

At this point, you and your team should be taking action and implementing your plan.

The launch *will* be exhausting. Hopefully it is also exciting for you.

Just hang in there and keep track of your progress. You'll need to continually improve on what you are doing as you go, but it's really the end of the campaign that you need to evaluate what you have done and how it can be improved.

Oh, did I not mention the end of the campaign? Don't worry, the next chapter will clarify when your campaign should "end" and what the next steps are.

MODULE 3

Refining Your Strategy

Without continual growth and progress, such words as improvement, achievement, and success have no meaning.

—BENJAMIN FRANKLIN

By continually improving their processes, Toyota became one of the world's biggest automakers. This happened by improving their operations as a manufacturer, but the same can be applied to your marketing.

Any time we decide to stop growing and improving, we stop being competitive. And in arguably the most competitive business environment ever, we need to make sure our competitive advantage is clear.

We do this by continual improvement.

I know that after all the effort you put into building a strategy, you want to take a break and rest. You have some time for that while you execute the strategy, but it doesn't end there.

You need to revisit what you've done and how it went. Then, you can make smart decisions on how to adjust your strategy to improve it next time around.

This is how you grow, improve, and ultimately, take command of your market. The real power comes in making these changes.

In the following chapter, you'll see how I recommend you do this. As a bonus, you'll also see that it's incredibly easy to iterate and change. Now that you have a strategy in place and a formula to use, it's easy to get great work done.

With that, let's see where you are after executing the strategy and what's next for you.

7

The Fifth Step – Recap & Review

Study the past if you would define the future.

—CONFUCIUS, ancient Chinese philosopher

Introduction

Congratulations! You built a strategy from the ground up, implemented it, and now the results are rolling in. You're far ahead of 99% of others out there!

So, now it's time for you to review how everything went.

I can just about promise you, despite all your hard work, it wasn't all rainbows and sunshine.

There were problems. It was exhausting. And, things didn't go as planned.

That's to be expected. Especially if this is your first time.

In this chapter, we're going to do a deep dive on all of these issues. To start off, we want to be sure you know *when* your campaign ends.

Maybe you already determined it, but if not, give this first section a read. You need to know if this is the right time to do a full recap, after all.

My Campaign's End

All great things have to come to an end.

You should set a deadline for when you want to consider your campaign over. This deadline might be clear cut if you have experience in this area, or you had a certain set number of months you would do your new advertising plan.

But if not, if your strategy had to do with one-off projects like building landing pages and installing new technology, it might be less clear.

If this is the case, set a deadline to call the project "complete" after a few months. They say it takes 9 months for marketing to start working. But, that was before the digital era.

In my opinion, three months after you finished launching the new campaign is a good time to review the results. A very minimum to end a campaign would be about two months. At most, I'd suggest nine months. Of course, you'll be checking in frequently to improve also.

Plan for what feels right to you. It could be two or nine months. There's no blanket answer - just make sure that you give your initiatives enough time to make an impact.

What worked?

You should have your records up to date with all the information relevant to each marketing activity: traffic generated, leads generated, revenues generated, and so on.

So now, where did you see the greatest ROI? What numbers brought you closer to your ideal state?

If there were any outliers that worked exceedingly well, it would be a good idea to invest more heavily into those areas. You also want to understand *why* they worked so well, so don't take them for granted. For example, it may not be the fact that you used Facebook advertising, but it may be the copy of that specific ad or the landing page used.

What didn't work?

There are also things that didn't work out so well. It's bound to happen.

Similarly, there may be areas that you feel time, energy, and money went to waste.

If you did find that happened, can you identify the cause? Can you cross-reference the potential weaknesses with the activities that did show positive ROI?

How would you adjust?

This is why tracking is so important. Over time, we can refine and adjust to make sure our money is spent in the most effective and efficient way possible.

For any business seeking growth, whether a million-dollar small business or a billion-dollar enterprise, you want to know how your business spends its money and how each area is serving you.

Calculating ROI on Social Media

I find social media to be one of the hardest channels to track ROI of. Yet, so many still are eager to jump on social media.

As such, I thought we'd talk about social media and how you can measure ROI. It's a popular question.

#1 - Set Your Goals

This is something we covered for the overall campaign, but make sure you have goals set for your social media activity. You might communicate this in another way, like specifying reach, traffic, leads, new customers generated, and customers serviced.

Remember that each conversion, whatever type it is, should have a monetary value attached to it.

Examples of Goals:

- Purchase
- Fill out a form
- Get a quote
- Sign up for newsletter
- Click on specific link
- Download PDF file
- Spend X minutes on specific page
- Share your page
- Like or Follow your page
- View video
- Visit blog

#2 - Choose the Right Platform

Not all social networks are made equal. You already defined your ideal customer profile, so you should know what network to be on and which would waste your time. Don't add more networks expecting greater results!

- B2B: LinkedIn
- B2C: Facebook
- Millennials: Twitter, Instagram
  Middle-Aged Females: Pinterest
- Foodies: Instagram, Pinterest
- Google employees: Google+

#3 – Track Campaigns

Again, tracking! There are different tools out there to help you track analytics of your chosen social network (just use Google for a list of a bunch of options). Most networks have built-in analytics, but you can opt for investing in more robust options if you feel the need.

#4 – Review, Recap, and Improve

Did you find what you were looking for? Did you generate all the leads you wanted and service enough customers for this investment to make sense?

Social media can be an intense undertaking, exhausting your time, energy, and money. Tracking ROI can help you determine if it makes sense for you, but remember to include the time and energy expenses as well. (Specifically, calculate fees, labor hours, labor cost, and the cost per social network.)

And as a final measure, look at the ROI:

ROI = [(Benefits – Investment) / Investment] * 100

For Benefits, you want to include a variety of elements. How much traffic was sent to your site from social media? How much of that traffic then converted into leads or customers? Were there any sales directly resulting from social media use?

Also, what benefits did you find in improving your brand? Did social media involvement increase your search engine ranking, leading to more organic finds? I don't believe you can set a specific dollar amount to this, but it's worth being mindful of when looking at ROI.

Now that was just a small overview of tracking ROI on social media, but did you notice something?

It parallels what this entire book has been about: prepare, plan track, and improve. You see, the strategy framework I show you in this book can be extended to other areas, like social media marketing.

Lessons Learned?

It's always nice to review the intangibles as well…

What did you learn from all of this? There was certainly a lot to do to prepare an effective strategy and roll it out.

I'm sure you learned a lot about your business: who your ideal customer is, what your business stands for, where you want it to be in the future, how you can get there, and what marketing works well (and what doesn't!).

But I'm sure there's more to it…

What did you learn about yourself? How patient are you? Can you grasp the big picture but not lost track of the actions that get you there? How was managing a project team and communicating the benefits to everyone? How did you develop as a leader?

I wrote this book to help people develop strategies, but over time I came to realize that it was more than that. This is an exercise to help ourselves grow as marketers, professionals, and individuals.

It's a huge undertaking and requires the type of commitment and dedication rarely found in most people.

But you did it. You read through every stage of this book, learned what you needed to, took action, rallied your team, kept yourself motivated, and put together an awesome strategy.

Congratulations.

You did it.

In this chapter, you learned:

- How to set a deadline for your campaign
- Determining what worked and didn't work in your strategy
- Analyzed how you might adjust for the future depending on the ROI you found
- How to calculate ROI for the elusive, and challenging social media marketing
- This wasn't an easy project to put together, but it shows your commitment

The journey is nearing its end, but not quite yet. There's a little more for you to read, and it is one of the most important points of this entire book.

I couldn't leave the book to end here. There has to be more to it, right?

There is, don't worry. Keep on reading and you'll find out what lies next for you...

8

Bringing It All Together

Alice said, "Would you please tell me which way to go from here?" The cat said, "That depends on where you want to get to."

- LEWIS CARROLL, author of Alice's Adventures in Wonderland

Introduction

I love it.

You made it so far. Further than most people will make it. I hope you're proud of yourself!

To quickly recap: we established where we are as a business and where we want to be, as well as the steps to get there. Then we took those steps and analyzed what worked and didn't work.

Now what's next? C'mon, you know the answer…

Next Steps

Start over.

That's right, go back to the beginning of the book when we start developing the chapter and do it all over again.

You see, this book is a framework. A framework should continue to be used, developed, and evolved for your company.

There may be parts of this strategy development you see that are too complex for your needs, or lacking in specificity.

Whatever the case is, you are becoming the expert now. I give you full permission to take what I gave you and customize it for your business and needs.

You're going to be better than ever now. You have experience with this strategy and can use it again. You know what worked and failed with your first strategy. It can only get better.

So get to work, please. And if at any time you feel stuck, reach out to me: David@PrimalDM.com I'd love to be helpful to you.

80/20 Rule Revisited and Reapplied

Earlier in the book, we talked a bit about the 80/20 Rule. You know that it says 20% of your input leads to 80% of your output.

And this has been proven among a variety of disciplines - mathematics and engineering, marketing and sales, software and risk management.

Did you see it in the results of your marketing? Take a look around and see where it might apply.

My suggestion is to consider doubling down on that 20% that gave you 80% in return. It's proven to work, so take advantage of the opportunity.

At the same time, you have room to cut underperforming initiatives, or at least significantly change them.

Don't simply focus on the one thing that's really working for you. Make sure to continue experimenting as well. If you go through much of this process again, you can think of different areas that may need focus and experiment there. Not enough demand? If social media failed and Google AdWords championed your efforts, why not give content marketing a try?

In this chapter, you learned:

- What to do after you complete the 5-steps of your strategy
- How to contact me if I can be helpful to you

Please do take me up on the offer to be helpful. I can't promise an immediate response, but I will do my best to answer each and every person that reaches out to me.

Besides, if I see anyone with specific questions regarding the book, I can always revise and improve on it. I welcome any criticism as well. It's often the best way to determine how to improve.

Sincerely,
David J. Bradley

Conclusion

Thank you again for investing in this book!

I hope this book was able to help you to develop a digital marketing strategy that brought you closer to your business and will bring you closer to your vision.

I hope you would share your results with me as well. I'd love to hear about your successes and be helpful if I can in any way.

Finally, if you enjoyed this book, then I'd like to ask you for a favor. Would you be kind enough to leave a review for this book on Amazon? The creation of this book took time and money, but most of all, an incredible amount of energy. A review would be greatly appreciated!

Thank you and good luck!

Before you go...

One more thing…

Remember in the beginning of the book you had a quick, 7-question survey? Well, it's that time again. I want you to see how you rank now, compared to before you went through this book and learned the concepts that helped you form a solid strategy.

And I'm really interested in your results. If you can, shoot me an email at David@PrimalDM.com with your before-and-after scores. I'd love to see what areas you really benefited in.

Do you have a digital marketing strategy? (A detailed plan, written out?)				
No – 0	1	2	3	4 – Yes
We do tactics like email marketing and social media, but no plan.	We know we need a plan, but nothing is in place yet.	We have strategies on some channels, but not overall.	Yes, focused on gaining visitors and converting them into leads.	Yes, we have a plan that includes all our marketing.

Do you track analytics, goals, and key performance indicators?				
No – 0	1	2	3	4 – Yes
We generally leave it to what's worked traditionally.	We check on traffic and keep an eye out for lead increases.	We use Google Analytics, but don't keep track of KPIs.	We use analytics and track goals, but something's missing...	Yes, we use goals, analytics, and KPIs. It's clear how they work together.

Do you speak to a general audience (opposed to a specific, ideal customer)?				
No – 0	1	2	3	4 – Yes
We focus on our products and services. They speak for themselves.	We know generally who we sell to. That's good enough.	We focus on certain targets specifically.	We created a detailed outline of who the buyer is.	We have an in-depth profile of our ideal customers and focus on them.

Do you have a digital sales funnel clearly defined and in use?				
No – 0	1	2	3	4 – Yes
We have salespeople who handle that.	Our phone number and "contact us" form is online so customers can reach us.	We have a rough framework, but we need to build on it.	We spent time developing the digital sales funnel, but not an entire digital strategy.	We have a complete digital sales funnel that integrates with our strategy.

Do you periodically review your digital strategy to improve it?				
No – 0	1	2	3	4 – Yes
We don't have a strategy to review!	We don't have any schedule to review. We will notice when we need to.	Part of our annual plan is to check in on this. I wouldn't say we "set it and forget it".	We constantly work on it, so a schedule isn't set but we think about it.	Our team has a set schedule to check on our strategy and continually improve it.

Are you happy with your budgeting for your digital marketing?				
No – 0	1	2	3	4 – Yes
It gives me headaches trying to decide on a budget, or stick to one.	We set budgets, but that doesn't mean we stick to them.	I feel like we limit ourselves with our budgeting.	We have budgets set up but are unsure if they are best for our needs.	We set smart budgets based on need and performance – all goes well!

Are you positioned well in your market, while making that clear to clients?				
No – 0	1	2	3	4 – Yes
We give info as to who we are... That's about it.	We give information about our products/services offered.	Some web pages explain why we are great to work with.	We try a bunch of messages to communicate our benefits.	Yes, we speak to our ideal customer, in a clear, well-positioned way.

Now, add them up and calculate your total. Where do you land?

0 – 7: Still pretty weak! What happened? Are you sure you did all the exercises? I think you might need some help getting over whatever challenge you're facing. Reach out and we can have a quick chat.

8 – 14: Not a ton of traction quite yet… If you haven't done all the exercises in the book, I'd recommend you start there. They can really make everything much more effective. If you *did* do that already, what's the issue? Reach out and let me know – I'll see how I can help.

15 – 21: Nice! This is a pretty good score – as long as you weren't higher than this before starting. Remember, 1% improvements make a huge difference, separating the good from the great. Keep working on gradual improvements. Slow and steady wins the race.

22 – 28: Hoo-rah! You did it, my friend. I'm not sure where you started, but where you're at is impressive. Not many people get to this point, so I really would like to congratulate you. If you found a certain section or concept especially useful, why don't you let me know? Feedback is appreciated!

Again, David@PrimalDM.com.

BONUS

A Copywriting Crash Course

Copywriting is an art form that can benefit people in almost every area of life - personal and professional.

Essentially, it is an emotionally-charged way of communicating that engages the reader and helps guide them through an extended decision process.

The decision process starts with reading the first line, to the second line, to the third, to having a desire build inside them, to taking some action.

It can certainly be a powerful skill, so it is worth developing.

But don't be scared of it being "manipulative". I mean, the purpose is to guide someone towards a decision, so it may be possible to be manipulative, but as long as you have a quality product and customers who need it, you aren't manipulative. You're helpful.

Here are a few guiding principles for your copywriting process:

- Don't worry about editing. Just empty all your thoughts down, even if they are horrible. The miraculous work won't happen if you worry too much about what you are writing down right now.
- Speak to your ideal customer. Create a profile and study it. Get to know them and how they think.
- The goal of the first sentence is to make the reader want to read the second sentence. The goal of the second sentence is to make the reader want to read the third sentence… and so on.
- Offer evidence in the form of testimonials, case studies, and social proof.
- Focus on specificity over generalities. It makes you more believable and becomes easier to connect with others.
- Take breaks. Your miraculous breakthrough will come when you're at the gym, in the shower, or stuck in traffic.
- Never stop learning (see below).

And for the words you write:

- Focus on benefits rather than features.

- Think about the emotions that go along with the reader at this point of their buying process.
- Be personal and human, using words like "I" and "We" as opposed to "the company" or "Company ABC". Avoid technical lingo.
- Use white-space, 1-2 sentences per paragraph, headings and subheadings. All have the purpose of breaking up large blocks of text into easily readable and easily scanned content.
- Be concise and clear. I like to use a tool called Hemingway App for this (http://hemingwayapp.com). (Generally, the lower the readability grade the better.)
- Make your headlines compelling (more later in the book on this).

To continue developing your copywriting skills, I recommend the following:

- *The Irresistible Offer* by Mark Joyner
- *Tested Advertising Methods* by John Caples
- *The Robert Collier Letter Book* by Robert Collier
- *Breakthrough Advertising* by Eugene M. Schwartz
- *Advertising Secrets of the Written Word* by Joseph Sugarman
- Get swipe files (copywriting work done by the pros) and rewrite them by hand. Spend

> 30-minutes each day doing this for a month. You'll see at the end you are much better at writing just as they do. (Don't type out the messages and don't quit after a few days!)

A popular framework to use in copywriting, marketing, and advertising is the AIDA model. If you're not new to marketing, you probably heard of this before.

AIDA = Attention, Interest, Desire, Action

One of the reasons this acronym has been around for so long is because it works. It works in so many different ways, and yes, despite all the changes in the last few decades, it works for digital marketing as well.

Keep in mind that getting attention, building interest, creating desire, and spurring action lies in one powerful tool: copywriting. This is just a framework – the skill has to be developed regardless.

BONUS

Practical, Simplified Neuromarketing

My passions and interests are a mix of topics such as psychology, communication, neuroscience, emotional intelligence, and marketing. And with the field of Neuromarketing quickly rising, I thought I'd share a quick, practical lesson.

Did you know we have *three* brains? It's true.

1. **Our old brain.** It's also commonly referred to as our reptilian brain. This dates back to our primitive days. Think 400 million years ago. It's home to our most basic functions, but a key function as well: deciding.
2. **Our middle brain.** This is where we process emotions and feelings. This is something we

tend to target in marketing, hoping it will influence our old brain.

3. **Our new brain.** We can also call this our logical brain. It's where we process data and rationally consider situations. If you've heard of the Neocortex before, that's part of our new brain.

What's this mean to us as marketers? We need to focus on reaching that old brain. That's where the decision to buy is made.

We usually try to build logical cases, listing out our features. If we're savvier, we use emotional triggers, discussing benefits. But persuasion can be better when targeting the old brain.

There's a ton of ways to target the old brain. Here's a list of ideas:

- Use pictures
- Use storytelling, and use it well
- Use stark contrast to make a point
- Communicate with emotion and passion
- Use testimonials and case studies as proof
- Always use the word "you" to focus attention on the reader or listener

These things all get the attention of the true decision maker within us. The logical and emotional points help to influence our old brain, but directly speaking to it gives us the greatest chance of success.

For an in-depth analysis of what's really possible with Neuromarketing, I recommend reading the book

Neuromarketing by Patrick Renvoise and Christophe Morin. They put together a great resource on how to practically use Neuromarketing. I just wanted to give you a sample so you know to keep an eye out for this rising methodology.

Acknowledgements

First, I want to thank you for reading this book. My readers give me an outlet to help people beyond those I can work with in a direct way. For my friends with entrepreneurial spirits, I hope this book helped you find success and continues to do so.

Now, I want to thank my family for inspiring me to live a great, fulfilling life:

David Bradley, Sr - a.k.a. Dad; you taught me everything about hard work and dedication. Without those lessons, this book would never come to fruition. Ginger Bradley - a.k.a. Mom; you help me see the light side of life to keep on laughing each and every day. Lisa Bradley - a.k.a. my big, little sister; you are full of energy and creativity that I hope to grasp just a bit of each day.

To my cousin Eddie Fleury, who has remained my best friend since before I can even remember. My future wife, Sahonny Nunez, who endlessly supports my dreams. My adorable puppy, Toaster, who delayed the publishing of this book but brings me so much joy.

To my grandfather, Antonio Biondi, who I miss dearly. My aunt, Maria Asermely, who never stops being a source of happiness, inspiration, and love, even when faced with life's greatest challenges. Auntie Frannie, thank you for making sure Eddie and me were well fed through our day-long video game marathons over the years. And to my entire, loving family, thank you for your support.

It wasn't just family, however. There are both friends I know and mentors I never met that I am grateful for. Some of these inspirations include the following:

Tim Ferriss, who is an amazing writer, marketer, and entrepreneur. I fell in love with his love of experimentation from when I first read *The 4-Hour Workweek.* Scott Britton, who introduced me to Business Development and continues to produce amazing personal development content. And Sam Ovens, who helped me along in starting my digital marketing consulting by sharing his successes and challenges.

Thank you to Chandler Bolt, James Roper, and Tyler Wagner for helping me learn how to self-publish a book that people really want to read. Ryan Holiday, for writing a powerful and concise overview on Growth Hacking, plus his newsletter that includes amazing books that keep adding to my bookshelf.

Noah Kagan and Neil Patel: these guys share the best, actionable digital marketing tips of anyone I've discovered. They are legends in what they do and relentlessly share what they know to help others. And let's not forget James Altucher, who shares practical advice from raw stories of his life. He's incredibly wise and yet humble.

And to a few more people that I know personally

Rick Day, my business coach and a mentor who helped me get my business off the ground. Without his accountability, I'd have a tough time staying focused and my first gaining clients. Larry Wilson, you were a great teacher and mentor to me, but also an amazing friend who I could always count on.

Thank you to Malane Thou, who was my first intern and team member at Primal Digital Marketing. He's an incredibly creative, young entrepreneur and complete rock star. And Tara Bryne, for connecting hundreds of young entrepreneurs in the Under 30 Changemakers group that I'm honored to be part of.

Digital Marketing Glossary

A/B testing - A/B testing is exactly what it sounds like. You develop two versions of something (a site or product), show them to people, and see which does better (A or B?). Tools like Qualaroo, Optimizely, KISSmetrics, and almost any landing page service will let you do this. The purpose: to get closer to the ideal method of communication.

Above the Fold - This refers to the visual content first seen when visiting your site. Essentially, it is what is seen before the user starts to scroll. While still important to consider, the variety of devices used to access websites today makes this less relevant than it previously was.

Analytics - Collecting and analyzing data from your digital marketing. Frequent analysis includes traffic, page visits, and page engagement. When checking analytics, beware of vanity metrics.

> **Vanity metrics** - Metrics that feel important, but are superficial or deceiving. They may be tied with ego or just ignorantly irrelevant. A common example is traffic to your website, without regard to engagement, bounce rates, and quality of traffic. Another key element: the metrics aren't actionable and don't translate well to ROI.

Traffic - The amount of visitors to a website.

Autoresponders (Email Nurture Sequences) - Also known as email nurture sequences, autoresponders allow you to automate your communication with leads and customers. Depending on the sophistication of the software you use, you may be able to trigger autoresponders to begin based on certain user actions or events. As a result, you are able to send the right messages at the right time, maximizing the impact of your communication.

Bounce rate - Something you want to minimize… When someone visits your website, a percentage will immediately leave. That percentage is your bounce rate. High bounce rate means something is wrong and you aren't engaging your visitors (or, you have low quality visitors). You can track this well with Google Analytics.

Call Tracking - The act of tracking calls made through your website by mobile visitors. It is popular for visitors to use your web page to find your phone number to call, so why not track where those calls come from (PPC, SERP, a certain page), rather than having to just assume?

Content Marketing - This is sometimes used interchangeably with inbound marketing. Others (like myself) see inbound as a philosophy, where content marketing is the actual creation, distribution, and promotion of content that fits within your inbound strategy.

Copywriting - Using words to design compelling text (copy). The purpose is to guide the reader towards what you wish, usually ending with a specific action (CTA).

> **Call-to-Action (CTA)** - A CTA is created to motivate the viewer to take a specific action. It is a fundamental tenet of copywriting. CTAs commonly lead to newsletter signups, opt-in forms for content, or "contact us" forms.

> **AIDA** - An acronym used in copywriting to form engaging messages: Attention, Interest, Desire, Action.

Cost Per Click (CPC) - CPC is the cost you are charged each time someone clicks on your ad. It is not affected by views (impressions); only clicks.

CRM (Customer Relationship Management) -

Conversion - A conversion is simply the result of a certain action being taken. It is commonly presented as when a lead becomes a customer, but a conversion can also take place with other calls-to-action, like newsletter signups.

Email Broadcasts (or Blasts) - An email sent out to your database without highly specific segmentation or personalization, nor an individual trigger to spur the broadcast.

Email Deliverability - The percent of messages delivered to recipients intended to contact. In other words, it excludes email bounces due to errors, incorrect addresses, and so on.

Guest Blogging - The purpose of guest blogging is to share audiences for visibility and SEO purposes. Whether you are the host or guest blogger, it can benefit you through exposure to a new audience, building authority, and SEO ranking.

Hashtags - A keyword or short phrase (without spaces) preceded by a pound sign (#) in social media posts. The purpose is to keep the conversation around that hashtag easily found and focused, using that hashtag. It is popular on Twitter primarily, although most other social networks use it as well.

Heatmapping - These tools give you a visual representation of how visitors interact with your website. It allows you to see what the popular areas are, as well as what areas are neglected. It's a great tool to optimize the user experience and find potential issues.

Ideal Customer Profile (ICP) - Our ICP is created as an in-depth outline of who we would most want to work with. This includes who is good for us financially, strategically, and personally. Aspects will include what motivates them, demographics, beliefs, and problems experienced. The more exact we can get, the better the ICP serves us when we target these ideal customers.

Inbound Marketing - Inbound is a marketing strategy and philosophy where rather than "pushing" our message on prospects, like traditional and display ads tend to do, we create compelling messages and content that attracts our ideal customers. The purpose of each message we craft is to engage, entertain, and educate.

Landing Page - A web page used in digital marketing that gives visitors two options: take the proposed action or exit the page. It removes all navigation and distractions from the central message to make the choice (your proposed action) more likely. Great copywriting makes the difference between a great and average landing page.

Lead Generation - The use of marketing to take potential customers, like website visitors, and turn them into leads. This is commonly done by gaining their contact information in exchange for a newsletter or content that will benefit the visitor.

Lead Magnets - Free offers you make to get a visitor's contact information in exchange. It is a way to offer value, build trust, and continue the conversation by collecting information, like an email address.

Marketing Automation (Lead-to-Revenue Management [L2RM]) - Marketing automation (or L2RM) is one of the fastest growing areas of marketing today. The software platforms and technology allow marketing (and sales) to learn more about their prospects, market to them on multiple channels, and automate marketing actions. When used properly, marketing automation can drive sales and prove ROI for many businesses.

Mobile-Responsive Design - Website design that results in pages resizing based on the device used to access them (computer, tablet, phone). The purpose and result is a more-fitting design and increased usability.

Organic Facebook Reach - The number of Facebook users that see your posts without your having to pay to sponsor (or "boost") the post. This is generally extremely low, so don't expect much better than around 10% of your following to even see your posts.

Pay-Per-Click (PPC) - Paid advertising on search engine results pages. You are charged each time someone clicks on your ad, rather than on impressions (views). It is the only way to instantly be ranked high on SERPS, compared to a long-term strategy like SEO. PPC can also include social media ads and retargeting.

AdWords - The advertising platform lead by Google. It accounts for much of the Pay-Per-Click (PPC) advertising online.

Bind Ads - This is essentially Microsoft's answer to Google's PPC system, AdWords. The advertising network is far smaller than AdWords, but by incorporating Yahoo's network, they still receive unique users and often cost far less than AdWords ads.

Responsive Web Design - See *Mobile-responsive design*.

Social Media Ads - Simply any advertising taking place over social media. Facebook is the most common channel to advertise on and arguably has the most sophisticated targeting system. Almost all social networks have advertising potential, so discover which best fits your needs and budget.

Retargeting - Also known as remarketing, retargeting is a new form of advertising online. The premise is that your ads can "follow" a visitor (or even someone you email) for an extended period of time by tracking them. For example, if someone visits your pricing page, you can set retargeting to track them when they go on various websites or social networks so that your ads appear there as well for days or even weeks after their visit.

Search Engine Optimization (SEO) - The practice of positioning a website on the SERP in as high a ranking as possible for a certain search term/query. It refers to the overall search engine strategy, incorporating on-page and off-page SEO elements.

SEO-related Terms:

Black Hat SEO – Search engine optimization can be manipulated, at a risk. Black hat SEO is using those risky, unethical, and illegal (according to Google's guidelines) techniques to try to increase your rank on the search engine results page (SERP). The opposite is, of course, white hat SEO. Think stuffing keywords and buying links. Any legitimate business should avoid this.

Gray Hat SEO –It's not the most simple to determine, but these are essentially the SEO practices between white hat and black hat SEO. Google's guidelines may touch on the general idea of these techniques without giving specifics. Gray Hat SEO is when you push the boundaries of what you can get away with. For the general business audience, I'd recommend you avoid this.

Keyword – A word or words you would align your content to so that search engine users can find your relevant material. In SEO, you use keywords to optimize your search engine rankings. In PPC, keywords are similarly used to optimize your ad placement.

Keyword Research – The process of researching what your ideal customers are searching for. Research helps you to ensure you are reaching your ideal customers while avoiding non-customers. There are multiple options for keyword research, with the most popular being Google's Keyword Planner.

Keyword Stuffing - Using more keywords than you need to in your content. An old black hat SEO trick. Don't do it.

Long-Tail Keywords - Keyword phrases that include multiple keywords for high accuracy when used in search engines and PPC advertising campaigns. They lower irrelevant searches, increase relevant searches, and generally result in smaller costs.

NAP (Name, Address, Phone Number) - Your NAP details should be consistent throughout the web for better SEO results, especially for local businesses.

Organic Search Results - Your links displayed on the SERP (search engine results page) due to a customer searching a query relevant to you. The opposing is paid search results, which comes in the form of PPC campaigns using Google AdWords or Bing Ads.

Off-Page SEO - Actions taken outside your website to increase its ranking on search engine results pages. This is commonly done through link building (linking to your site form other sites), guest blogging, and with social media.

On-Page SEO - Actions taken on your website to increase its ranking on search engine results pages. This is commonly done by using relevant keywords, ensuring keywords are used in your copy, and setting parameters search engines care about (like title tags, internal links, image optimization, and so on).

Search Engine Results Page (SERP) - The SERP is the results page on a search engine like Google or Bing based upon the query searched. It's an aspiring goal to be the first ranking on the SERP, but a challenging task that's sometimes not worth the resources.

White Hat SEO - SEO practices that are confirmed to abide by Google's guidelines (as well as other search engines). They are generally ethical, valuable, and not deceptive. This is what you should focus on as a reputable, trusted business seeking long-term growth.

Sales funnel - A series of steps to find prospects, turn them into leads, nurture those leads through their buying process (or your sales process), and convert them into customers.

Attracting Traffic - It would be nice if we could set up a website and just have our ideal clients roll in. Unfortunately, that doesn't happen, so we need a plan on how to attract traffic. That is the first step of the sales funnel, and it may include things like advertising, social media, and content marketing.

Capturing Leads - Once we do have traffic coming to our site, we need to do something with it, or else it's all lost. That's why we need to capture leads by creating lead magnets that give us prospect contact information, turning visitors into leads.

Nurturing Leads - Now that we have contact information on our lead, we can continue the relationship. This is when we walk alongside the lead and help them find how we can solve their problems and benefit them. This may be through marketing automation, autoresponders, and more.

Converting Leads - Finally, we have our leads that are now educated and ready to buy, so let's help them do that. A strong call-to-action while acknowledging objections will help us get there. That's what we do in this stage, when we convert lead into customer.

About the Author

David Bradley is the founder of Primal Digital Marketing. Born and raised in North Providence, Rhode Island, he decided to develop a business that would serve his communities in Rhode Island and through the global connection of the internet.

Driven by an intersection of passions in emotional intelligence, communication, psychology, technology, neuroscience, and marketing, David's purpose is to help others realize their growth potential and experience the benefits of effective and efficient digital marketing.

David studied Marketing and Operations Management at Rhode Island College, where he joined the Emerging Leaders program, frequented the Dean's list, and graduated Cum Laude and a Presidential Scholar.

He went on to pursue his MBA focused in marketing at Providence College where he served as a Business Education Innovation fellow, developing a scenario-based project, "Leadership Styles in Decision Making", for MBA students and an undergraduate colloquium.

Made in the USA
Middletown, DE
02 February 2015